SMALL LIBRARIES
ORGANIZATION AND OPERATION

THIRD EDITION

DONALD J. SAGER

HIGHSMITH PRESS HANDBOOK SERIES

Highsmith
PRESS
Fort Atkinson, Wisconsin

Published by Highsmith Press LLC
W5527 Highway 106
P.O. Box 800
Fort Atkinson, Wisconsin 53538-0800

Cover and illustrations by Mary Ann Highsmith.

The paper used in this publication meets the minimum requirements of
American National Standard for Information Science —
Permanence of Paper for Printed Library Material. ANSI/NISO Z39.48-1992.

ISBN 1-57950-058-7

Contents

1. **Introduction**   1
   What Is a Library?
   Who Manages the Library?
   History
   Libraries Today
   Goals of Effective Library and
      Information Service

2. **Planning**   7
   What Is the Purpose of the Library
   Determining the Scope of the Collection
   Usage
   Determining How the Collection Should Be Organized
   Determining Needed Space
   Defining Needed Skills and Human Resources
   Budgeting
   Evaluating Effectiveness

3. **Ordering Library Materials**   14
   Selection Policies
   Resources for Selection
   Order Procedures
   Using Computers

4. **Organizing the Collection**   20
   Simplified Cataloging
   Simplified Classification
   Cataloging in Publication and Preprocessed Materials
   Levels and Types of Processing for Library Materials
   Computerized Catalog Systems
   Dealing with Donated Materials
   Organizing Pamphlets, Magazines and Other Print and
      Nonprint Materials
   Alternatives to Cataloging and Classification
   Weeding

5. **Processing and Lending**   29
   Library Materials
   Preparing Books and Other Materials
      for Loan
   Binding, Repair and Preservation
   Circulation Systems and Procedures
   Library Borrowers Cards
   Circulation Procedures
   Overdue Fines
   Supplies

6. **Designing the Efficient and**   36
   Attractive Library
   The Program
   Furnishings
   Environmental Concerns
   Selection and Purchase of Library Equipment
   Selection of Architects and Consultants
   Maintenance
   Protecting the Library

7. **Reference and Information**   42
   Services
   Reference Interview
   Answering Reference Questions
   Selection
   Reference Networks
   Interlibrary Loan Networks

8. **Borrowing Resources from**   49
   Other Libraries
   Union Catalogs
   ILL Code
   Delivery
   Costs
   Partnerships with Other Libraries

9. **Serving Your Users**   53
   Children and Young Adults
   Adult Services
   Services to Persons with Disabilities
   Outreach
   Measurement and Evaluation

10. **Your Library's Human**   58
    Resources
    The One-Person Library
    Adding or Replacing Staff
    Evaluating Performance
    Resolving Personnel Problems
    Volunteers

11. **Developing Your Library**   64
    Start With a Vision
    Financial Development
    Marketing and Promotion
    Publications
    Signage

Tours
Exhibits and Displays
Events

12. **Small Public Libraries**   **71**
The Mission and Objectives of the Public Library
Governance and Relationship to Local Government
Public Library Policies and Procedures
Public Library Finance
Legal Requirements
Typical Services and Organizational Structure

13. **Small School Libraries &**   **76**
Media Centers
The Role and Responsibilities of the School Library/Me-
    dia Center
Relationship to School Administration and Faculty
Legal Requirements
School Library Budgeting
School Library Policies and Activities

14. **Special Libraries**   **81**
Church and Synagogue Libraries
Law Libraries
Business Libraries
Medical, Health Sciences, and Institutional Libraries
Institutional Libraries
Museum and Historical Society Libraries

Appendices

A. **State & Provincial Library**   **88**
    Agencies

B. **Dewey Decimal Classification**   **90**

C. **Library of Congress**   **91**
    Classification System

D. **Interlibrary Loan Form**   **92**

E. **Library-Related Resources**   **93**
    on the Internet
    Selecting a Computer for the Internet
    Connecting with the Internet
    Training for the Internet
    Selected Resources

F. **A Library Promotion Calendar**   **97**

    Index   **98**

Introduction

Chapter 1

The purpose of this handbook is to provide an introduction to the organization and operation of a small library for those who do not have formal training in library and information science and for relatively new librarians who need basic guidance in managing a small library. Emphasis is on practical direction in the development of library services, resource collections, and user policies. Care has been taken to eliminate jargon, and to include clear examples and creative solutions to common problems, with many additional sources listed at the end of each chapter. Small libraries are defined in various ways—by the size of their collection, number of users, volume of usage, staff size, among other factors. For the purpose of this book, however, small libraries are those with collections of less than 25,000 books or other resources, a staff of less than ten, and a potential clientele of less than 5,000 persons.

The third edition emphasizes the increased use of computers and the Internet to save time and improve service. Also, a summary of the core values that serve as the foundation for library service has been added. All the resource lists have been updated, including the websites. Each chapter has been revised to include practical advice on new information resources, how to apply new national standards to improve user services, and where to make needed changes in the physical design of the library. Additional features include a library promotion calendar, time- and cost-saving suggestions from the Frugal Librarian, and new special websites that will be of exceptional value to the managers and staff of small libraries of all types.

To further add to the practical value of this handbook, brief suggestions identified as **"Advice from the Frugal Librarian,"** appear throughout the book.

The initial chapters of this handbook will introduce the basic library operations common to virtually all types of small libraries, and subsequent chapters will briefly discuss the organization and operation of a small library in specific settings. A practical approach will be stressed throughout this guide, and suggestions will be made at the end of each chapter on resources an individual may consult or organizations that may be contacted for assistance in dealing with more specialized problems.

Some recognition should be given to *How to Organize and Operate a Small Library* by Genore H. Bernhard (Highsmith, 1975). This brief publication was developed by Highsmith Inc. in response to frequent requests from the many institutions that regularly purchased their supplies and equipment from the Company's catalogs. The trust and confidence established through these relationships led to frequent requests for advice on a wide range of services and problems. Ms. Bernhard's guide provided many library staff with the concise and clear information they needed to effectively serve their clientele, and it was revised several times before it was retired in 1991.

Because of the many changes which have affected library service, an entirely new handbook was written in 1992, and revised in 1996 and 2000. It is intended to reflect contemporary library and information science philosophies of service and more effective use of new technology and standards of practice. However, it employs the same straightforward, basic advice that provided guidance to a generation of individuals who were given responsibility for the formation and administration of their organization's library. It is also assumed that the individual who uses this manual will have to be resourceful in organizing and managing the library because they will have limited staff and funding. Because of these constraints, this handbook offers alternative policies and procedures to save time and funds, whenever possible.

What Is a Library?

Libraries are defined as a collection of resources, carefully selected and organized, to provide information to contribute to the mission or activities of an institution. firm, community, school or other entity. The resources may consist of books, magazines, correspondence, computer tapes or disks, photographs, recordings, or any other form of information. It is important to realize that a library does not have to possess a collection of books to fulfill its function. What distinguishes a library is that it has been developed and largely organized to permit its users to conveniently retrieve information that will aid them in their work, or enrich or educate them

Libraries are often called a variety of different names, reflecting the needs of the organization they are intended to serve. A business may call its library an information center. Schools may refer to their library as an instructional materials center. Certain social service agencies may designate their library an information and referral service. For simplicity, we shall refer to these units as libraries in this handbook, although it is important to remember that the designation the organization uses for its library is critical in defining its role.

Who Manages the Library?

The individual who is responsible for the organization and operation of the library may have a variety of different job titles, depending on the nature of the organization that supports the library. Sometimes this individual may be called a librarian, even though he or she may not have the formal training the title suggests.

Different nations have various academic requirements or standards for librarians, although it is often common for a professional librarian to have postgraduate training at an institution of higher learning, in a program

Core Values

There are many different types of libraries, serving a variety of organizations and users. The individuals who staff and manage these libraries possess various skills and training, and they perform diverse services to aid their users. Despite their different roles and background, the library's staff have the following values in common:

Connection of people with ideas and knowledge.

Assurance of open access to intellectual resources.

Commitment to literacy and learning in all its contexts.

Defense of everyone's irrevocable right to form and exercise one's own beliefs.

Respect for the individuality and the diversity of all people.

Preservation and interpretation the human record.

Excellence in professional service to our communities.

Formation of partnerships to advance these values.

(ALA. Core Values Task Force. Preliminary Draft: Core Values, Chicago: ALA, 2000)

accredited by a professional association or some unit of government. For example, in the United States, professional librarians are generally considered those persons who have completed a postgraduate program accredited by the American Library Association. States and provinces may also impose licensing requirements, and professional status might be granted based on completion of a specified sequence of coursework, years of experience working in a library, or some combination of training and experience.

In a school setting, this individual may be called the school media specialist. Some businesses and social service organizations refer to this individual as their information services coordinator. In many smaller businesses and agencies, responsibility for the library may be one of several assignments given to an individual, and the job title may reflect those duties. For simplicity, in this handbook we will refer to this individual as the manager. Whatever the level of training or experience this individual possesses, she or he will have considerable responsibility to effectively organize and administer the entity's information resources, and that is a management function.

History

Libraries are as old as recorded knowledge. The first prehistoric cave paintings constitute a library of sorts, recording events that were important to the tribe. When language evolved into a form that was more portable, libraries consisting of these records were formed. The ancient Egyptians maintained libraries of rolls of papyrus, an early form of paper, which may be seen in many museums. The Greeks and Romans also established libraries which preserved the greatest writings of their era. Most of these libraries were destroyed during the Dark Ages, but scribes carefully transcribed the works of Plato, Socrates and other great classical philosophers, historians, poets and others for posterity.

In the Middle Ages, libraries were limited in number, being the property of kings and the Church. Scholars in the great universities had access to small libraries, but the books were so few and precious that they were often chained to the shelves. The invention of printing with movable type by Johann Gutenberg in the fifteenth century, the coming of the Renaissance to Europe, and the development of a more educated populace led to an increase in books and the subsequent creation of large national and university libraries.

Libraries were also created in the Far East, where paper was invented and developed. Books were printed with blocks, and beautifully illustrated scrolls were preserved as national treasures. In the Americas, the Maya and other early civilizations carefully recorded their history and their scientific discoveries on temples and other public buildings. These libraries of stone are now providing scholars with insight to the greatness of these societies. On the African continent, libraries were preserved in many forms ranging from the papyrus records of the Egyptians to the exquisite engravings of many of the great tribal empires.

In colonial America, the church played a major influence in education and the formation of libraries. Many frontier ministers carried their personal libraries with them, and shared these with the members of their congrega-

Professional Licenses
Some states and provinces may require individuals who wish to earn or retain a professional license to take examinations or continued training, a practice common in many other professions. To determine whether a license or any other requirement exists to manage or establish a library, contact your state or provincial library. A complete list can be found in appendix A.

Benjamin Franklin is generally credited as being one of the founders of the American public library movement, with the establishment of the Philadelphia Library Company in 1733. This library was supported by subscription fees charged to library members, and many other communities soon borrowed this idea.

tion. The belief in free public education led to a more literate population, a strengthening of democracy, and a parallel growth in libraries.

The concept of free public libraries supported by taxes—spearheaded by active women's organizations, the philanthropy of Andrew Carnegie in creating over 2,000 libraries throughout the United States and the world, and universal free public education—eventually led to the present network of over 3,600 college and university libraries, 17,000 public libraries, tens of thousands of special libraries of all types, and over a hundred thousand school libraries in the U.S., as well as parallel growth throughout the rest of the world.

Libraries Today

We live in an information age. Knowledge and technical expertise are among the major exports and imports in commerce today, and intellectual property is as respected and valued as industrial and agricultural products were earlier in the nineteenth and twentieth centuries. Advances in printing, photocopying and other forms of photographic and electronic reproduction have made it possible to disseminate cultural, scientific, business and technical information rapidly and economically throughout every nation and across national borders.

However, the sheer volume of information threatens to drown society in an avalanche of unneeded material, to frustrate users seeking access to specific information, and to harm the environment due to the consumption of resources required to fuel the information age. The key is a logical process of selection and organization of information based on a sound understanding of user needs. That is the basis for library and information science today.

Libraries were originally created to preserve recorded knowledge at a time when it was relatively rare. They evolved during the eighteenth and nineteenth centuries, functioning as distributors of what were still relatively costly resources. While there is still a role for libraries in the preservation and dissemination of knowledge, it is increasingly more evident that libraries today, particularly small libraries, have a much greater role in the selection and organization of information. Because of the sheer volume of knowledge and the cost of selection and organization, it is increasingly more important for small libraries to specialize and share resources.

The computer and new evolving forms of information offer great opportunity to aid small libraries, but they also present some new challenges. Just as the invention of the printing press made it possible to preserve and more economically disseminate information, the computer makes it theoretically possible to record and distribute everything, instantly and cheaply, anywhere in the world. New forms of information makes it possible to store and transmit immense quantities of data. By the middle of the twentieth century, more than a quarter million new book titles were being produced each year throughout the world, including over 50,000 in the U.S. alone. The computer now makes it possible to bypass the normal book distribution channels, and information is increasingly being marketed in electronic and optical form.

The manager of yesterday's small library had to master the Dewey Decimal Classification System, learn how to type and file catalog cards, and identify the best source for library supplies and books. Today's manager must be able to select the best database management system, learn how to use a growing set of

Role of the Small Library
The sheer volume of knowledge and the cost of selection and organization makes it increasingly more important for small libraries to specialize and share resources than to try to collect and preserve everything their users require.

online computer files, index and catalog a wide array of resources, understand where to go and how to use a growing network of libraries for needed information, and be able to select more sophisticated supplies and information in a host of formats. Today's library manager is at the center of a revolution in how a firm or institution perceives its role in society. Whether the organization is nonprofit or for profit, it must continuously research its users' needs, plan for a future that is forever changing and more complex, and where the speed at which it can change is likely to affect its ability to survive.

Goals of Effective Library and Information Service

While the emphasis of this handbook is on the practical rather than the theoretical, every library manager must begin the organization of the collection and the design of library service with some clear understanding of what is to be achieved. The next chapter describes some practical steps on planning specific goals and objectives, but before that process can be initiated, the manager must have an understanding of the purpose of the firm or institution the library serves, who its users will be, and what type of information they will be seeking.

Libraries are not static collections. They change continuously, and it is just as important to know what to discard as to acquire. The needs of the library's users continuously change. While some questions may be the same, it is more likely that the small library will never receive the same question twice. It is also likely that the user who seeks information from the library will know more about the subject than the manager. However, that user may not know how that information is organized in the library, or the other related subjects that should be consulted. Therefore it is important to always keep the goals listed below at hand when planning for library services.

Goals of Effective Library and Information Service

1 To keep the library's collection and service relevant.
Maintain a close correlation between the mission and goals of the firm or institution and the library. For example, just because a company once sold taxidermy supplies doesn't mean the company library should always maintain a collection on the topic.

2 To know the library's users and their needs.
Continuously reevaluate who uses the library, for what kind of information, and devise a method for determining whether they are really getting the information they require.

3 To know the library's limitations.
In today's increasingly more specialized society, no library is ever large enough to provide all the answers to user needs. Know where other resources can be obtained, and plan the library's collections and services accordingly.

4 To keep current with trends in library and information service.
It will not be possible for the manager to maintain the effectiveness of the library, unless that individual maintains his or her awareness of what is occurring in the field.

Further Resources

Associations

The following associations can provide services and resources to help in the organization of a small library. Write or call for membership information:

American Association of Law Librarians, 53 W. Jackson Blvd., Ste 940, Chicago, IL 60604. Tel: 312/939-4764; Fax: 312/431-1097; E-mail: aallhq@aall.org; Web: www.aall-net.org

American Library Association, 50 E. Huron, Chicago, IL 60611. Tel: 312/944-6740 or toll-free 800/545-2433; Fax: 312/440-9374; E-mail: wgordon@ala.org; Administrative.Services@ala.org; Web: www.ala.org

Canadian Library Association, 200 Elgin Street, Ste. 602, Ottawa ON K2P 1L5 Canada. Tel: 613/232-9625; Fax: 613/563-9835; E-mail: cla@www.ca; Web: www.cla.ca

Church and Synagogue Library Association, Box 19357, Portland, OR 97280. Tel: 503/244-6919 or toll free 800/LIB-CSLA; Fax 503/977-3734; E-mail: csla@world accessnet.com; Web: www.worldaccessnet.com/~csla

International Federation of Library Associations, POB 95312, 2509 CH, The Hague, Netherlands. Tel: 011 31 70 3140884; Fax: 011 31 70 3834827; E-mail: IFLA@ifla.org; Web: www.ifla.org

Library Association, 7 Ridgmount Street, London WC1E 7AE England. Tel: 011 20 7255 0550; Fax: 011 20 7255 0500; E-mail: info@la-hq.org.uk; Web: www.la-hq.org.uk

Medical Library Association, 6 N. Michigan Ave., Ste. 300, Chicago, IL 60602. Tel: 312/419-9094; Fax: 312/419-8950; E-mail: info@mlahq.org; Web: www.mlanet.org

Special Libraries Association, 1700 18th St., NW, Washington, DC 20009. Tel: 202/234-4700; Fax: 202/265-9317; E-mail: sla@sla.org; Web: www.sla.org

A comprehensive listing of more specialized associations, as well as state and provincial library associations can be found in *The Bowker Annual Library and Book Trade Almanac* (New Providence, NJ, R.R. Bowker).

Periodicals

American Libraries. This is the monthly journal of the American Library Association, which is the largest and one of the oldest associations in the world devoted to libraries of all types and sizes. It contains articles on trends and news of the latest developments in the field. For subscription information contact: American Library Assn., 40 E. Huron St., Chicago, IL 60611 USA

Bulletin of the Medical Library Association. Covers trends in the health sciences field for librarians. For subscription information contact: Medical Library Association, 6 N. Michigan Ave., Chicago, IL 60602 USA

Canadian Journal of Information and Library Science. Articles on library service in English and French Canada. For subscription information contact: University of Toronto Press, 5201 Dufferin Street, Downsview, Ontario M3H 5T8 Canada

LA Record. This is the official journal of the Library Association (United Kingdom), containing articles, reviews, and news on trends. For subscription information contact: Library Association, 7 Ridgmount St., London WC1E 7AE England

Library Journal. This is published 19 times a year, and it contains news reports and general articles on trends. It also contains extensive reviews of new books, periodicals and media on a variety of subjects. For subscription information contact: Library Journal, 247 W. 17th St., New York, NY 10017.

Special Libraries. This is the official journal of the Special Libraries Association, containing articles on trends, news from the field, and reviews. For subscription information contact: Special Libraries Association, 1700 18th St., NW, Washington, DC 20009

Teacher Librarian: The Journal for School Library Professionals. Formerly *Emergency Librarian.* Practical articles and reviews for school and youth librarians. For subscription information contact: Teacher Librarian, Box 34069, Dept. 284, Seattle, WA 98124-1069

State Library Agencies
See appendix A for a complete listing.

Selected Books on Library History
Harris, Michael H. *History of Libraries in the Western World.* 4th rev. ed. Metuchen, NJ: Scarecrow Press, 1995. 309 p.

Martin, Lowell A. *Enrichment: A History of the Public Library in the United States in the Twentieth Century.* Lanham, MD: Scarecrow, 1998. 224p.

Wiegand, Wayne A. and Donald G. Davis, eds. *Encyclopedia of Library History.* New York: Garland, 1994.

Library magazines are extremely valuable resources for keeping current on the latest trends, but small libraries may not be able to subscribe to all the appropriate titles. The Frugal Librarian suggests that the managers of nearby small libraries pool their resources and route several of the less frequently consulted titles.

Planning

Chapter 2

It's been said that if you don't know where you're going, any road will take you there. It definitely applies to organizing a library. Planning a library can be one of the most rewarding experiences an individual can ever have, since the resources and services the library offers will be of continuing benefit to the library's users. However, it can also be a frustrating and disappointing experience without proper planning. The intent of this chapter is to provide some basic suggestions to the individual who has been given this responsibility, and needs practical advice.

What Is the Purpose of the Library

Whether this is a new library, or one which was previously established, ask the individual or group who has given you the responsibility for organizing and operating the library two questions:

* What is the purpose for the library?

* How will it relate to the mission or purpose of the firm or institution it serves?

This may seem self evident or obvious, but do not take it for granted. All organizations have changing goals. What the firm manufactures today or in the past, may not be what they will be doing tomorrow. If the firm is planning to develop new products, the library may be required to support research and development on those products and a new market.

Many times a rudimentary library collection may already exist, even when a new library is being started. Individual officers in the institution may have collected materials in their own offices. Correspondence and other records may be in files which are to become part of the library's collection. Again, do not use these to determine the scope and nature of your future collection. They may deal with yesterday's concerns and issues and have only limited utility for the future.

If one does not already exist, ask that an advisory committee be formed to help in planning the collection and service. The committee should be

Statement of Purpose for a School Media Center

The purpose of the Jones Elementary School Library is to support the instruction provided by the faculty, and enrich learning by the students, working in cooperation with other area libraries.

Statement of Purpose for a Corporate Library

The purpose of the Smith Corporate Information Center is to provide management and staff with technical, business and marketing information to support its current product lines, and to contribute to research and development of new products and services.

broadly representative of the different types of users the library will serve. This will provide better insight into who is expected to use the library, and for what purposes. One of the committee's first responsibilities should be to assist the library manager in preparing a statement of purpose, or in reviewing any existing mission statements, so that there is a clear understanding of the library's role in the institution.

Determining the Scope of the Collection

The advisory committee and a user survey *(See side-bar)* can help in defining the collection. However, many libraries of all types and sizes prepare a ***collection development policy*** to serve as a reference. Generally the policy contains the mission or purpose of the library, subjects that will be emphasized, subjects of secondary interest, and sometimes, subjects which will be specifically avoided. This policy is important in making decisions on budget, and in assessment of gifts. It will also be important in estimating initial and future space and equipment needs. For example, if this is a church library, and it is determined that the library will purchase everything published by the church's denomination, it should be possible to determine publishing output on an annual basis.

Another element in the collection policy will be the range of the publications in terms of currency. For example, the policy may be to keep the ten most recent years of the most popular magazines in the field, or to keep technical literature which is no older than ten years. The manager may decide to use judgment on selected titles, depending upon user needs. However, if the library begins to run out of space, this policy will provide a basis for discarding materials from the collection.

Collection Development Policy

Mission statement
Primary subject focus
Secondary subject interests
Materials _not_ collected
Currency of materials

Developing a Questionnaire

Another suggestion, depending on the size of the organization the library will serve, is to develop a simple questionnaire or survey form to be distributed to the library's users. Among the questions that should be asked are:

1. What types of subjects and materials should the library collect?

2. How current, or how far back do these materials need to go?

3. What should be the hours of service?

4. What type of services are expected from the library?

5. Do users currently obtain information and resources from other libraries? Do they plan to continue using these libraries? (If so, ask for the names of these other libraries and the type of information used.)

There may be many other questions you or your advisory committee may wish to add. However, please aim at keeping the survey brief, and only seek the answers to questions that will help you in planning the library and its services. Evaluate the results, and plan on repeating the survey at regular intervals in the future to compare the results and to identify changing needs.

Usage

Another aid in determining the size and scope of the collection is usage. Record should be kept of the circulation or loan of materials by classification or subject. If the library uses one of the computer-based circulation systems that are currently available through a reputable library supplier, it may be possible to obtain these statistics automatically. If the library uses a manual circulation system to keep track of who borrows library materials, statistical information may have to be maintained with a simple manual record by loan category. If your library loans a large number of materials, a periodic sampling of loans may provide an estimate of how often certain categories of books are borrowed. More information on statistics will be provided later in this chapter and in chapter 5.

Another way to determine the size, scope and nature of the collection is to visit other libraries and to ask for a copy of their collection development policy, particularly if the library is similar in purpose. Every state has a state library agency, and they usually maintain statistical information on all types of libraries located in the state. A complete list of these agencies is in Appendix A. Some states also have regional library agencies designed to support cooperation and resource sharing among libraries of all types. Some of these agencies, called multitype cooperative library systems, or simply systems, offer consultant assistance which might be available at no cost. The state library agency can provide information on the availability of this assistance.

Determining How the Collection Should Be Organized

Many persons might think of the library classification system they learned in school when they give any thought to how a library should be organized. In fact, there are a number of related concerns—such as whether all the resources should be segregated by type of material (i.e., books and magazines), or perhaps whether materials should be segregated by user type (i.e., technical and professional)—that are just as important as classification in improving user access.

Although most persons learned how to find books in their school, public or college library using either the Dewey Decimal Classification System (DDC) or the Library of Congress Classification System (LC), there are many other alternatives the manager can choose in organizing the library collection. For example, a photographic library might be organized simply by subject or name. There are a large number of special classification systems devised for special types of libraries, such as churches, law or medical libraries because of inherent weaknesses in the DDC or LC systems. There simply is no universal way to organize the collection.

Once again, the needs of the users and the nature of the materials in the collection will provide the best guide. Either the advisory planning committee or the user survey can provide valuable insight, as will a visit to a similar library. Generally, it is best to avoid special classification systems or unusual methods of organizing the collection because they are alien to the way in which persons learned how to use libraries. Moreover, a special organization system may require the manager to devote more time to training the users how to find materials. It is also possible to purchase some materials already cataloged and classified if a standard classification system is selected. Ultimately, the decision should always be based on what is most convenient to the user, and provides the best access to the collection and information it contains.

Some libraries can afford a consultant to aid in planning a library. However, the Frugal Librarian suggests an alternative if funds are limited. *The American Library Directory* (Bowker, Annual) lists many types of libraries by geographic location, and provides comparative statistics such as collection size and budget, as well as the names of key staff, major telephone numbers and addresses. *The World Guide to Libraries* (K.G. Saur, 1995) is similar in nature for international libraries. While no two libraries are likely to have exactly the same type of users, there may be enough commonalities to merit a visit, and one of the library's staff may volunteer some assistance.

Determining Needed Space

Whether the library manager is assigned a specific location for the library or given the opportunity to select an area, it is important to prepare a plan for the library based on a written program. A program is simply a written description of the purpose and functions of the library, and an estimate of the square footage and equipment that will be required. More information on this can be found in chapter 6, but it is important that the manager begins with the realization that a library is not just a place possessing shelves, books and other resources. It is a service which is based on satisfying its users' needs, and that it is designed not for storage but for convenience of access.

Assuming the manager has defined the purpose or mission of the library, the next responsibility is to identify the functions required to support user services. A typical small library is likely to have Collection Management, User Services and Administration functions, as shown in the side-bar here.

Typical equipment to support these functions would include shelving, filing cabinets, a desk and/or table for processing materials, and similar furnishings. The catalog of a reputable library equipment and supply firm should provide information to what is available, and a visit to a similar library would provide practical insight into how it is used. More information will be found in chapter 6 on how to estimate the space requirements and cost of this equipment. Computer software is also available from reputable library supply firms and computer stores to simplify space planning.

Defining Needed Skills and Human Resources

It is assumed that the reader of this guide is likely to be either the only person operating the library, or at best, the manager of a small staff. Regardless of the size of the staff, good planning requires the definition of skills requisite for the initiation and operation of the library. This will be essential for the identification of needed training, selection of consultant assistance, or decision to contract for regular supportive services.

The library needs to develop three elements to define needed skills and human resources:

- Schedule of hours,

- Organization chart, and

- Job descriptions.

It is also assumed that the library's mission is clearly defined, and relates to these three elements.

Organization Chart: The organization chart is a diagram of the library's functions, and it is useful for even a one- or two-person library because it will serve as a guide in the allocation of time, and a basis for adding future staff as the library grows in usage and responsibility.

Job Description: The job description is a summary of the requirements for each position in the library, including education and experience, and a sum-

User Services Functions

Collection Management—This includes processing and housing the library's resources (i.e., books, files, recordings, etc.).

User Services—This includes the area and equipment the manager and staff require for serving library users, as well as tables, seating and special equipment dictated by the nature of the collection.

Administration—This includes all other space required to support the operation of the library, which might consist of the manager's desk or office space, computer storage, supply closets, or a staff rest area.

Staffing Needs

Assuming that the library's hours of service exceed the manager's scheduled working hours, additional staff will be required. The volume and nature of user requirements will also affect how much time a single individual would be available for assistance. Typically, a smaller library with a specialized function gives a more intensive and individualized level of user service.

mary of typical duties. Even in a small library where one or two people may be responsible for doing everything, it is desirable to prepare job descriptions. This will be useful in determining compensation, workload, and additional training requirements. If the library uses part-time personnel or volunteers, it will also help in defining where work can be allocated. Chapter 10 provides additional guidance in planning personnel requirements, and sample job descriptions can be found in several of the resource books listed at the end of that chapter.

Budgeting

Every library requires a budget, regardless of its type or size. This will consist of income and expenditures. Many small libraries will have only one source of income, and that will be an allocation from its parent institution or company. Others may have supplemental income from gifts, charges to users, endowments, or contracts for services. In some libraries, the manager may not have any responsibility for handling either revenues or expenditures. An accountant or bookkeeper may be responsible for paying bills or developing financial reports.

It is essential, however, for every library manager to develop a budget based on anticipated expenditures and to either maintain or monitor regular financial reports on revenues and expenditures. This may be a shared responsibility with others in the organization, but it is a fundamental administrative requirement.

Budgets are developed based on historical information (i.e., the library's budget in former years) or upon projected usage and development, or a combination of the two. The library manager may either be allocated a specific income level by the organization's budgeting authority and expected to design expenditures to fit within that allocation, or receive an allocation based on a budgetary request. Usually the budgeting process is well defined and will require justification to upper management for any additional funds the library manager requests. The development of a logical plan for the organization and operation of the library, preferably over a period of three to five years, is a major aid in justifying the budget, since it allows upper management to see how and when the funds would be used.

There are numerous ways for budgets to be organized, but the most common method is called "line item budgeting," which lists expenditures by subject. The following is an example:

ITEM	AMOUNT LAST YEAR	PROPOSED AMOUNT THIS YR
Personnel	$15,000	$15,750
Books & Other Matls.	10,000	11,000
Supplies	3,600	4,000
Utilities	1,200	1,400
Equipment	2,000	2,000
Travel & Trng.	500	600
Other	250	250
Total	**$32,550**	**$35,000**

In developing an initial or new budget, the library manager should always confer in advance with upper management to identify any guidelines. If there will be limited income for growth, or perhaps reductions, this should be taken into consideration in developing the budget request. Nonetheless, the library manager should take initiative in identifying ways in which the library can improve its services to users, even though it might increase budget requirements. For example, increased purchases of books will help make users more efficient. The manager should also bear in mind the relationship between the different elements in the budget, in addition to the impact of inflation on costs of operation. The purchase of additional books compared with the preceding year, for example, will require additional supplies for processing, and possibly additional shelving. Checking current supplier catalogs will provide a basis for estimating these costs.

Evaluating Effectiveness

Another primary responsibility of every library manager is the evaluation of effective performance, and this should be planned as a part of everyday operation.

Many libraries keep statistics on the loan of materials or the number of users they have assisted. This may be manually maintained or collected and analyzed by computer, if the library uses appropriate software. It can also be collected on a sampling basis. This is helpful as a justification for budget requests, and an aid to selection of materials and determination of hours of service. While this is certainly appropriate, there may be other important activities which require measurement and evaluation.

This manual has stressed the importance of planning, and one important measure of effectiveness is the progress the library has made in achieving its goals and objectives. Operational statistics may indicate that the library is busy, but it may not be effective due to the continued use of obsolete equipment or an out dated collection. This manual has also stressed the importance of a focus on user needs.

Another method for evaluating the effectiveness of the library would be a periodic survey of library users to determine their satisfaction with service and the collection, and the identification of new services or materials. The advisory committee established to assist the library manager in planning should also advise the manager on how to monitor effectiveness.

Alternative Ways to Evaluate Your Library

- User surveys
- Numerical statistics
- Consultant observations
- Progress toward a stated goal
- Comparison to similar libraries

Resources

Internet Listservs and Newsgroups—If your library has the ability to access the Internet, it is possible to subscribe to a listserv (which is really an automated mailing list) or a newsgroup (a news distribution service) which can provide valuable information on library planning and problem solving. Listservs allow users to submit questions that can be addressed by a wider group of individuals interested in the same subject. See appendix E for a listing of library-related newsgroups and listservs.

State Library Agencies —See appendix A for a listing of agencies in the United States. These agencies have consultants who may be able to provide useful information in planning library service.

Cooperative Library Systems—Many states have cooperative or multitype cooperative systems serving specific regions of the state. The state library agency can identify these, and describe the type and level of service which is available. Frequently these systems offer specialized consultant assistance, interlibrary loan, training, back-up reference and referral, and other services.

Key Resource Books

American Library Directory (Bowker, biennial) This comprehensive reference tool, which should be available in larger public and academic libraries, identifies and briefly describes public, special and academic libraries. It is arranged by state and community, and it would be a good source of information on comparable libraries that could be contacted for assistance or resource sharing.

Eberhart, George, compiler. *The Whole Library Handbook 3: Current Data, Professional Advice, and Curiosa about Libraries and Library Services.* (ALA, 2000. 576 p.) This is a one-volume encyclopedia of miscellaneous facts about libraries, together with lists and noteworthy articles.

Legenfelder, Helga, ed. *World Guide to Libraries*, 14th ed. (K.G. Saur, 1999, 2 vols.) Similar to the preceding title, this is a directory of libraries of all types throughout the world, having collections of 30,000 or more. It is organized by nation, and it contains comparative statistical information, addresses and telephone numbers.

The Librarian's Yellow Pages (P.O. Box 179, Larchmont, NY 10538) This is an annual purchasing directory of all types of services and materials used by libraries. The main section is organized by subject, with a company name index containing addresses, telephone numbers, e-mail addresses, and websites.

Other Resource Books

Berk, Robert. *Starting, Managing, & Promoting the Small Library.* Armonk, NY: M. E. Sharpe, 1990. 160p.

Carson, Kerry D., et al. *The ABCs of Collaborative Change: The Manager's Guide to Library Renewal.* Chicago: ALA, 1997. 273p.

Hernon, Peter, and Ellen Altman. *Assessing Service Quality: Satisfying the Expectations of Library Customers.* Chicago: ALA, 1998. 256p.

Himmel, Ethel, and Bill Wilson. *Planning for Results.* Chicago: ALA, 1998. 328p.

Mason, Marilyn Gell. *Strategic Management for Today's Libraries.* Chicago: ALA, 1999. 192p.

McCarthy, Richard. *Designing Better Libraries: Designing and Working With Building Professionals*, 2nd ed. Ft. Atkinson, WI: Highsmith Press, 1999. 132p.

Nelson, Sandra, et al. *Managing for Results: Effective Resource Allocation for Public Libraries.* Chicago: ALA, 2000. 320p.

Prentice, Ann. *Financial Planning for Libraries.* 2nd ed. Metuchen, NJ: Scarecrow Press, 1995. 236p.

Reed, Sally G. *Small Libraries: A Handbook for Successful Management.* Jefferson, NC: McFarland, 1991. 156p.

Robbins, Jane, et al. *The Tell It! Manual: The Complete Program for Evaluating Library Performance.* Chicago: ALA, 1996. 272p.

Smith, G. Stevenson. *Accounting for Libraries and Other Not-for-Profit Organizations*, 2nd ed. Chicago: ALA, 1999. 336p.

St. Clair, Guy, and Joan Williamson. *Managing the New One Person Library*, 2nd ed. Bowker Saur, 1992. 192p.

Turock, Betty J., and Andrea Pedolsky. *Creating a Financial Plan.* New York: Neal-Schuman, 1991. 150p.

Advice from The Frugal Librarian

Managing a small library can be a lonely experience, especially if the staff consists of only one or two persons. One alternative some libraries have found helpful is to develop a sister library relationship. If you can locate a similar type in another country, it may offer an opportunity to share solutions to common problems, exchange resources, and borrow creative ideas from one another. The Internet makes it very convenient to communicate with other libraries, and there are no geographic or political barriers.

Assistance in finding a sister library can be obtained from the **National Commission on Libraries and Information Science (NCLIS)**, 1110 Vermont Ave., NW, Ste. 820, Washington, DC 20005-3552; Tel. 202/606-9200; Fax: 202/606-9203; Web: www.nclis.gov.

NCLIS has also developed a brochure on the Sister Libraries Program which can be accessed on the Web at <www.nclis.gov/millennium/slbooklt.pdf>.

Ordering Library Materials

Chapter 3

Library managers have many choices in the way they can order books and other library materials. There are many different sources, and time and money are only two of the factors to be considered in selecting reliable suppliers. The library manager should be aware of the specialized policies and procedures that are associated with ordering from them. Moreover, there are many helpful guides to building a library collection, and a host of selection tools that can keep the library manager aware of newly published books and other resources.

Selection Policies

As mentioned in chapter 2, it is of critical importance to have a written statement describing the nature of the collection the library is to develop. This selection policy will provide a reference when questions arise on what to purchase, and what to discard. It should be reviewed regularly, as the needs of users evolve. A number of helpful titles are contained at the end of this chapter which will aid in the preparation of a selection policy. However, the usual selection policy contains the following elements:

1. The mission or purpose of the library;

2. A description of the subjects the library will select, and the extent of the selection (i.e., *comprehensive*, or everything that is published on the subject; *selective*, or the best recommended titles; *representative*, or a more limited selection from among the best recommended titles);

3. A description of how long these resources will be retained (i.e., permanently, or for a specified time, such as five years);

4. A description of the types of materials or formats the library will collect (i.e., books, audiotape recordings, periodicals, etc.);

5. A summary of the subjects or formats the library will not collect;

6. A summary of the standards the library will use in the selection of its materials;

7. Procedures the library will use in considering recommendations for purchase or removal of materials from the collection.

There can be many other elements in a selection policy, depending on the mission of the library and the nature of the organization the library serves. The suggested readings can supply more information on these options.

Resources for Selection

There are many general sources the manager can use for selecting materials for the collection, but these may be more limited depending on the special nature of the library. In general, the following types of sources are available:

Recommended Buying Lists or Bibliographies: Many publishers and associations have developed comprehensive lists of books and other resources recommended for libraries of various sizes and types. For example, *The Public Library Catalog* (H.W. Wilson) contains an excellent range of titles appropriate for small and medium sized public libraries. Such bibliographies almost always contain the full bibliographic information for simplicity in ordering, and often they will include an annotation and reading level. Bibliographies for special types of libraries are listed in the subsequent chapters of this guide. One caution is that older bibliographies may contain recommended titles that are out of print, or no longer available from the publishers.

Starter Collections: Some wholesale book suppliers, or jobbers as they are often called, will provide an entire basic collection for new or expanding libraries. Often these collections can be purchased fully cataloged and ready for circulation, at an additional cost. *(A listing of major jobbers is contained at the end of this chapter.)* These starter collections, however, are usually available for only more common types of small libraries, such as schools and small public libraries. The library manager charged with responsibility for starting a new library may wish to check with local or major jobbers to determine what is available and at what cost. If a starter collection is purchased, the manager will need to carefully describe the types of materials and subjects to be supplied, their recency, and the budget. These specifications should be carefully reviewed with the supplier to ensure they understand what is needed, and the mission of the library.

Publishers' and Jobbers' Catalogs: All publishers and book jobbers will furnish copies of their catalogs. *Literary Market Place* (R.R. Bowker) contains a good representation of the major publishers, with their addresses and telephone numbers, and the manager can ask to be included on their mailing lists. One caution is that catalogs are unlikely to contain negative reviews, and the annotations may not necessarily be objective.

Selection Journals: The best resource for new and current titles are those periodicals that contain critical reviews of books and other resources. *(A listing of the most important selection journals is at the end of this chapter.)* More specialized selection journals are listed in the following chapters on specific types of libraries. Even though most journals maintain rigorous standards for evaluation, the library manager should exercise caution in relying solely upon reviews. Only a small percentage of new books are reviewed, and some delay may occur before reviews appear.

Advice from The Frugal Librarian

The Frugal Librarian suggests that an easier way to develop a catalog collection might be for the manager to attend the next state or national library association conference, and visit the exhibits. Many associations allow nonmembers to visit the exhibits without charge or for a nominal fee. Since many publishers, suppliers and other firms display their new books and products at these trade shows, it offers good opportunity to inspect new books, pick up catalogs, and establish contacts. The manager should bring extra business cards, or run peel off labels on the computer to avoid having to write the library's mailing address multiple times.

Order Procedures

Books and other library materials may be purchased from local bookstores, direct from the publishers, or through a library book jobber or distributor. Whichever source used, the library manager needs to use a standard order form, and include the correct bibliographic citation on the order form.

Some books use the same title, and there may be different editions available. Therefore, to avoid an error in ordering the wrong book, the library manager must ensure that specific information is contained on the order form. Most library materials/book catalogs contain standard order forms that provide for essential information such as author, title, copyright date, publisher, edition, price and a unique number known as the International Standard Book Number or ISBN. Magazines or books which are regularly reissued will have an International Standard Serial Number assigned (ISSN). Some computer software programs are available which will automatically generate order forms, and record the order for future reference. With this information, copied from the review or catalog, the manager can be certain that the correct book is ordered.

It is good practice to retain a copy of the order form, so that duplicate orders are not sent. Well-designed computer software programs, called acquisitions systems, will automatically store this information for future reference. If the library does not have a computer, then an on-order file should be maintained. Usually the standard order forms sold by library supply firms come in multipart carbon forms, which allow one copy to be sent to the jobber or publisher, and allow another copy to be filed for future reference when new books are received or ordered. The on-order form can be arranged in any preferred order, such as author or title, but a consistent order must be maintained.

Selecting a Source

While books and other materials can be ordered from several sources, the library manager should consider the relative advantages and disadvantages of the alternative sources.

Bookstores: Libraries often prefer to use a local bookstore because of the opportunity to examine books before purchase. Many bookstores will order titles they do not have in stock. The library manager should inquire whether the store will offer a library discount, and be prepared to indicate the budget available for new book purchases. The disadvantage of using a bookstore is that the discount is usually not as high as the other sources cited below, and the stock may be relatively small. Most smaller independent bookstores keep only a few thousand popular titles. The advantage of using a bookstore is the convenience, the opportunity to examine the book, and personal service. The larger independent booksellers and the chain bookstores may offer 60,000–100,000 books, music, video, and CD-ROM products.

Publishers: All publishers will either handle direct orders from libraries, or if they are smaller presses, refer the order to a fulfillment service capable of handling multiple publishers and orders. In dealing with either a publisher or fulfillment service, the library manager should always inquire about discounts. This will often vary depending upon the volume of copies and the types of books ordered. Because libraries are often the primary source of

If the Order Information You Have Is Incomplete

To obtain missing elements of a bibliographic citation or to verify the information already in hand, the manager should consult a very basic tool known as *Books in Print* (R.R. Bowker) or more commonly called *BIP.* This multi-volume set comes in author, title and subject sections, and it will provide valuable information for ordering, such as whether lower cost paperback editions or other versions are available. This reference tool is also available in electronic form and can be accessed online if the library has a computer with a modem.

orders for many specialized publishers (for example, 60 percent of all children's books are ordered by schools and libraries), a special discount rate is often available to libraries. The disadvantage in dealing directly with publishers is that there are over 25,000 of them, and locating their current address, and processing orders to multiple locations can be daunting. Addresses for many publishers can be found, however, in *BIP* or *Literary Market Place.*

Some of the larger library publishers have sales representatives who visit libraries to discuss new books, but these "travelers" are less common today because of the cost of keeping these individuals on the road. Moreover, they are likely to visit only the larger accounts. Some smaller publishers are using an alternative means of reaching libraries; they may negotiate with a distributor or a commissioned salesperson who will represent many different but complementary publishers. These sales representatives may be able to offer attractive discounts, and advance information on forthcoming titles. However, care should be taken to ensure the salesperson is an authorized representative, and record of the sales terms should be retained for comparison with the invoice.

Library Jobbers: Many libraries prefer to order all or a majority of their books and other materials from a wholesaler or jobber because of greater discounts, specialized services or the convenience of being able to order books by multiple publishers from one source. The amount of business libraries can give a jobber will determine the level of discount, and therefore, it may be an advantage for the library manager to cooperate with other libraries in negotiating a discount or reducing shipping costs. Many jobbers offer automated order systems, customized billing, selection guides, options which allow books to be received already cataloged and ready for circulation, and a range of other services which should be evaluated carefully by the library manager. Several of the major jobbers are cited at the end of this chapter, but there are other smaller jobbers that specialize in different types of libraries, or concentrate in different regions of the nation. The disadvantage in working with a jobber is that they do not stock every publishers' books, and that they may be too large to offer the customer service a smaller specialized library may require. Furthermore, jobbers may not be able to process orders for non-book materials. There are firms, however, that specialize in handling orders and processing for audiovisual formats for libraries, and their advertisements can be found in many library journals.

Using Computers

Depending on the volume of orders, the library manager can be burdened with a high volume of record keeping and bibliographic research in ordering materials for the collection. Even a library that orders only a small volume of new materials can experience a problem because of the details associated with ordering. For this reason, it is recommended that managers of any size library give careful consideration to the use of a computer to order materials. The advantage is that certain information used for ordering, namely the bibliographic citation, can be reused for cataloging and circulation control. The cost and source of the book can be readily determined if it should be lost or needs to be reordered.

Prepublication and Greenaway Plans

These plans are offered by some publishers, and usually feature attractive discounts.

In a prepublication plan a publisher will offer a discount prior to the scheduled publication date.

Greenaway plans provide all or specified categories of books that a publisher releases.

The disadvantage of either plan is that the books will usually be unreviewed. Some publishers, however, allow for return of materials libraries find unsuitable.

Back-Orders

When a publisher or jobber cannot immediately supply a book, they may inform the library that the item has been placed on back-order. When the book is available, it will automatically be sent. Since this may take anywhere from a week to several months, many libraries state on their orders that back-orders should be cancelled if they can't be filled within a specified time, such as 120 days.

The greatest expense the library will incur is personnel, and the smaller the library, the more valuable will be library staff time, especially in a one person library. While a computer may represent a significant investment, that expense can be justified if staff productivity can be improved. Computer equipment, software and supplies can be purchased from local stores and from library suppliers at very competitive prices, and the library manager should identify the equipment that is needed, and shop for the best price and service. Vendors of library-related software can specify the equipment that is needed for their application, and often they can recommend the best sources. Some will even offer a complete package of hardware and software. If so, the manager will need to compare the purchase price and maintenance charge with local prices and services.

More on the selection and use of computers in the library will be found in subsequent chapters, but it is important for the library manager to recognize that many functions in the library can be computerized to save time and money, and that software has been designed and is available at reasonable prices for this purpose. If the library manager and staff do not have experience with microcomputers, training would be a very worthwhile investment.

Time, Money and Labor Saving Suggestions

Besides using computers to save time and money, the library manager might consider the following alternatives:

1. Always negotiate with the book supplier for the best discount, but don't neglect to inquire about shipping costs and other services that might save time and money.

2. Analyze which publishers supply large numbers of titles selected for the library. Most publishers specialize in certain topics, and small special libraries may find that they are buying many titles from the same publisher. If so, consider an "on approval" plan with the publisher, which may represent an added discount and save time in ordering.

3. If the library subscribes to a number of periodicals, contact several of the subscription agencies that advertise in the library periodicals and exhibit at library conferences for a quote on the library's list. A discount might be available, and an agency can save time and money in renewals and claiming missing copies.

4. Consider purchasing books from remainder houses, particularly in building new collections. These are firms that specialize in taking books from publishers which have not sold, and offering them at substantial discounts. While caution needs to be taken, some books may be remaindered not because they are poor quality, but because the publisher did not adequately market them or may have overestimated the demand.

5. Before ordering a title, always consider the potential demand and whether the book can be borrowed on interlibrary loan from another nearby library. Remember that it is not the size of the collection that is a measure of quality.

Resources

Books In Print (R.R. Bowker, Annual) This is a multi-volume annual publication which is arranged in author, subject and title sections. It is very useful in verifying bibliographic information and determining the availability of books. A CD-ROM version is also available.

Literary Market Place (R.R. Bowker, Annual) This provides addresses, toll-free telephone numbers, and information on the special interests of thousands of major American publishers, as well as other book trade information. Two companion publications, ***International Literary Market Place*** and ***AV Market Place*** are available from the same publisher, and they offer similar information on major international publishers and producers/distributors of many audiovisual formats.

Bowker Annual Library and Book Trade Almanac (R.R. Bowker, Annual) This will provide facts, figures and reports of value to all types and sizes of libraries.

Major General Book Selection Journals

See Literary Market Place for a comprehensive listing.

Booklist, 50 E. Huron St., Chicago, IL 60611

Book Links, 50 E. Huron St., Chicago, IL 60611

Book Reviews on the Internet, 2323 Mapleton, Boulder, CO 80304 (e-mail sbrock@teal.csn.org)

CHOICE, 100 Riverview Ctr., Middleton, CT 06457

Kirkus Reviews, 200 Park Ave. S, New York, NY 10003

Library Journal, 249 W. 17th St., New York, NY 10011

New York Review of Books, 250 W. 57th St., New York, NY 10107

New York Times Book Review, 229 W. 43rd St., New York, NY

Publishers Weekly, 249 W. 17th St., New York, NY 10011

School Library Journal, 249 W. 17th St., New York, NY 10011

Books

ALA. ALCTS. ***Guide for Written Collection Policy Statements***. 2nd ed. Chicago: ALA, 1996. 40p.

ALA. ALCTS. ***Guide to Performance Evaluation of Serials Vendors***. Chicago: ALA, 1997. 45p.

Cabeceiras, James. ***The Multimedia Library: Materials Selection & Use***, 3rd ed. San Diego, CA: Academic Press, 1991. 316p.

Cassell, Kay, and Elizabeth Futas. ***Developing Public Library Collections Policies and Procedures: A How-to-Do-It Manual for Small & Medium Sized Public Libraries***. New York: Neal-Schuman, 1991. 143p.

Curley, Arthur, and Dorothy Broderick. ***Building Library Collections***. 6th ed. Metuchen, NJ: Scarecrow Press, 1985. 350p.

Eaglen, Audrey. ***Buying Books: A How-to-Do-It Manual for Librarians***, 2nd ed. New York: Neal-Schuman, 2000. 175p.

Evans, G. Edward. ***Developing Library and Information Center Collections***, 4th ed. Englewood, CO: Libraries Unlimited, 2000. 595p.

Futas, Elizabeth, ed. ***Library Acquisition Policies & Procedures***, 2nd ed. Phoenix, AZ: Oryx Press, 1984. 616p.

Hirshon, Arnold, and Barbara Winters. ***Outsourcing Library Technical Services***. New York: Neal-Schuman, 1996. 173p.

Katz, Bill. ***Vendors & Library Acquisitions***. Binghamton, NY: Haworth Press, 1991. 239p.

Kemp, Betty, editor. ***School Library & Media Center: Acquisitions Policies & Procedures***, 2nd ed. Phoenix, AZ: Oryx Press, 1986. 280p.

Whitehead, Robert J. ***A Guide to Selecting Books for Children***. Metuchen, NJ: Scarecrow, 1984. 323p.

SELECTED MAJOR BOOK JOBBERS

Baker & Taylor Books
2709 Water Ridge Parkway
Charlotte, NC 28217
Tel. 800/775-1800
Fax: 704/329-8989
E-mail: btinfo@btol.com
Web: www.baker-taylor.com

Blackwell's Book Services
6024 SW Jean Rd., Bldg. G,
Lake Oswego, OR 97035
Tel. 800/547-6426
Fax: 503/639-2481
E-mail: bridges@bname.
blackwell.com

Bookazine
75 Hook Rd.
Bayonne, NJ 07002
Tel. 800/221-8112
Fax: 201/339-7778

The Bookmen
525 North Third St.
Minneapolis, MN 55401
Tel. 800/328-8411
Fax 800/266-5636

Brodart Books & Services
500 Arch St.
Williamsport, PA 17705
Tel. 800/233-8467
Fax: 570/326-6769
E-mail: bookinfo@
brodart.com

Coutts Library Services
1823 Maryland Ave.
Niagara Falls, NY 14302-1000
Tel. 800/772-4304
Fax: 716/282-3831
Web: www.coutts-ls.com

Emery-Pratt
1966 W. Main St.
Owosso, MI 48867-1397
Tel. 800/248-3887
Fax: 517/723-4677
Web: www.emery-pratt.com

Follett Library Resources
1340 Ridgeview Dr.
McHenry, IL 60050
Tel. 800/435-6170
Fax: 800/852-5458
Books & AV for school libraries

Ingram Book Co.
1 Ingram Blvd.
La Vergne, TN 37086-1986
Tel. 800/937-8000
Fax: 615/793-3810
Web: www.ingrambook.com

Koen Book Distributors
10 Twosome Dr., PO Box 600
Moorestown, NJ 08057
Tel. 800/257-8481
Fax: 800/225-3840
Web: www.koen.com

Organizing the Collection

Chapter 4

One the primary objectives of every library is to improve the accessibility of the collection to benefit the users. A variety of cataloging and classification procedures and standards have been developed for this purpose. *Cataloging* is a process which is designed to describe an item, such as a book, in a fashion to facilitate ease of location. Identifying its author, title and subject headings, for example, is part of cataloging. *Classification* is the process of assigning a number, letter, symbol or some combination of these to a book or library article so that it can be shelved, filed or grouped together with similar or related materials. A number of basic texts are recommended at the end of this chapter for those who wish to study the standard and more specialized cataloging and classification systems for different types of libraries.

However, the best course for the manager of a small library is to employ a relatively simple cataloging procedure and adopt a standard classification system. The two most widely used classification systems employed in U.S. libraries today are the Dewey Decimal Classification System (DDC) and the Library of Congress Classification System (LC). The Universal Decimal Classification System (UDC) is used by many international libraries.

Most libraries today, of all types and sizes, buy or obtain their cataloging and classification from other sources, and employ a standard cataloging and classification system. There are several reasons for this: First, a specialized cataloging and classification system may be difficult for both the library manager and library's users to learn, and that will require more time. Second, it will be difficult if not impossible to purchase preprocessed materials in anything other than one of the standard classification systems. Third, staff time is the most expensive aspect of a library's budget, and any functions which are likely to be time intensive should be avoided. Another word of caution—never fall to the temptation of developing a unique cataloging and classification system for the library. While the individual who devises it may understand it, and believe that it will save time and money by avoiding the necessity to buy preprocessed materials or catalog information, that individual will not be at that library forever. A new library manager would then be forced to learn the unique system, or con-

Organization Alternatives
Librarians can organize their collections in any of the following ways:

By format: keeping similar types of materials together.

By classification: assigning a number or code to keep materials on the same subject together.

By alphabetical order: filing books by author names or magazine titles.

By user group: shelving books that are intended for a specific type of user, such as children, together.

Or by a combination of some or all of the preceding methods.

vert it, at great time and expense, into a more standard system.

    Despite these cautionary warnings, library managers will still need to learn and understand simple cataloging and classification, for it is not always possible to purchase this information from other sources. Locally produced materials, gifts, and information in unusual formats may not be cataloged or classified by other libraries, and this may require what is known as original cataloging.

Original Cataloging: When the library that owns an item undertakes its cataloging and classification, usually because there is not alternative source, it is called original cataloging.

Simplified Cataloging

In organizing the collection, the library manager will need to decide whether the library will have a computerized or a card catalog. While the traditional card catalog is more common in libraries today, that is rapidly changing as the costs of computerizing are coming down, and because of the many advantages of the newer technology. Fortunately, the same standard of simplified cataloging can be used in both instances.

    In simplified cataloging, it is standard practice to work directly with the book or other format, rather than a printed description or review, to ensure that the cataloged description is correct. If it is a book, it is advisable to work directly from the title page, and the following page, which contains the copyright information. Using a 3x5 card or slip of paper, the following information should be copied from the book:

Author last name, first name and middle name or initial. [From title page] Title, and subtitle, if any. [From title page] Series or edition, if any. [From title page] City of first publication. [From title page] Name of the publisher. [From title page] Copyright date. [From title or copyright page]

No. of pages. [From last no. page in book] Illustrations if any. [By checking] Bibliography and Index, if any. [By checking] Subject headings assigned. [Using *Sears List of Subject Headings* or others listed below]

Copyright page: Most book publishers will include information regarding the date a work was copyrighted and who holds the copyright on the page behind the title page of the book.

    The most widely adopted standard for library cataloging is the *Anglo-American Cataloging Rules*, 2nd edition (ALA), or *AACR2*, and it is cited in the bibliography at the end of this chapter. It should be considered for purchase, for it will provide complete guidance on more difficult books and other materials.

Subject Headings

Subject headings can be derived from various sources, but it is important to use one of the more standard tools. *Sears List of Subject Headings* (H.W. Wilson) is one of the most commonly used tools among many small libraries, and it is highly recommended. However, the Library of Congress also publishes its *Subject Headings*, which is listed at the end of the chapter. It is much more comprehensive, and it is the most common cataloging resource used in medium and larger libraries. Both books have extensive cross references (for See and See Also) which the library manager should incorporate in the library catalog.

Note: Card sets for the most common cross references are commercially available.

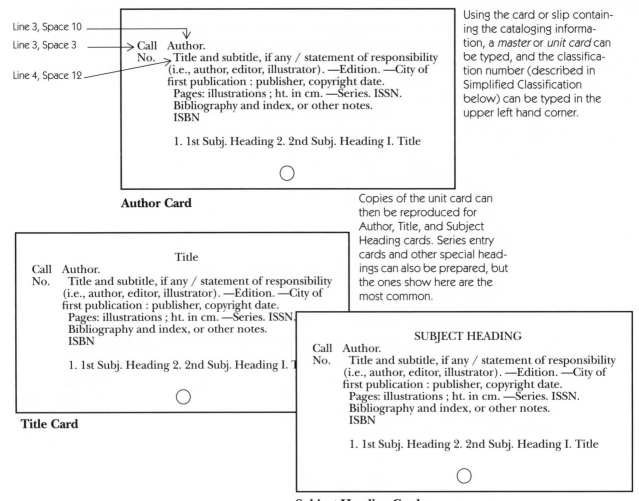

Line 3, Space 10

Line 3, Space 3

Line 4, Space 12

Call Author.
No.   Title and subtitle, if any / statement of responsibility
       (i.e., author, editor, illustrator). —Edition. —City of
       first publication : publisher, copyright date.
         Pages: illustrations ; ht. in cm. —Series. ISSN.
       Bibliography and index, or other notes.
       ISBN

         1. 1st Subj. Heading 2. 2nd Subj. Heading I. Title

Author Card

Using the card or slip containing the cataloging information, a *master* or *unit card* can be typed, and the classification number (described in Simplified Classification below) can be typed in the upper left hand corner.

                              Title
Call Author.
No.   Title and subtitle, if any / statement of responsibility
       (i.e., author, editor, illustrator). —Edition. —City of
       first publication : publisher, copyright date.
         Pages: illustrations ; ht. in cm. —Series. ISSN.
       Bibliography and index, or other notes.
       ISBN

         1. 1st Subj. Heading 2. 2nd Subj. Heading I. T

Title Card

Copies of the unit card can then be reproduced for Author, Title, and Subject Heading cards. Series entry cards and other special headings can also be prepared, but the ones show here are the most common.

                    SUBJECT HEADING
Call Author.
No.   Title and subtitle, if any / statement of responsibility
       (i.e., author, editor, illustrator). —Edition. —City of
       first publication : publisher, copyright date.
         Pages: illustrations ; ht. in cm. —Series. ISSN.
       Bibliography and index, or other notes.
       ISBN

         1. 1st Subj. Heading 2. 2nd Subj. Heading I. Title

Subject Heading Card

Simplified Classification

The two most widely used classification systems used in U.S. libraries today are the **Dewey Decimal Classification System** (DDC) and the **Library of Congress Classification System** (LC). The Universal Decimal Classification System (UDC) is used by many international libraries. Librarians are in disagreement regarding the relative advantages of these systems.

Dewey Decimal Classification System (DDC)

The DDC was developed by Melville Dewey in the nineteenth century, and it is based on a division of all knowledge into ten broad classifications, with multiple subdivisions, which are summarized in appendix B.

The DDC is periodically updated to reflect new disciplines and subjects, and it is among the most widely taught library classification system in U.S. schools today. Despite its relative simplicity, some librarians believe it has limitations for very large or highly specialized collections. Some special libraries that use the DDC have modified it to avoid these lengthy numbers. However, this is not recommended for small libraries because it is nonstandard. Both a regular and an abridged version of the DDC are available and are cited at the end of the chapter.

While the DDC has the capability to adjust to special classifications, the classification number may tend to become so long that it is difficult to place it on a book spine. For example, the DDC classification for a book on electronic publishing is **070.50285**.

Library of Congress Classification System (LC)

The Library of Congress Classification System (LC) was developed at that institution because of the sheer size and complexity of its collection, and it is commonly used in larger academic and more specialized libraries. Like the DDC, knowledge is divided into a number of broad categories, and then subdivided into specific subjects, using a combination of letters and numbers. A summary of the broad letter categories appears in appendix C.

Because of this combination of letters and numbers, the classification number is not as long as DDC classifications for newer and more specialized materials. Since it was more recently developed, some librarians believe it is inherently better for classification, but that is by no means universally accepted.

Universal Decimal Classification (UDC)

The UDC is similar to the DDC in its structure, but it has been modified to permit more classifications for the history, culture, and geographic features of other nations of the world. There are many other classification systems, and some are described in the texts at the end of the chapter, but the DDC and LC classification numbers are the ones most commonly available in purchased cards for U.S. libraries.

Cataloging in Publication and Preprocessed Materials

One of the most popular programs launched by the Library of Congress to benefit libraries is its "Cataloging in Publication" plan (CIP), which allows publishers to submit manuscripts and bibliographic information to LC in advance of publication. Through this plan, the publisher receives cataloging information back from LC, which it can include in the book. This CIP information appears on the copyright page of the book, where it can be used by those libraries that wish to reproduce it to generate their own cards or enter it into their automated catalogs.

While the CIP information may be incomplete— it does not include, for instance, the length or size of books—or other information on the book may not be available, it provides a majority of the information needed for cataloging. Unfortunately, not all publishers participate in this program as yet, but the number is steadily increasing.

Libraries that have access to the Internet and the World Wide Web (WWW) have the added option of searching LC's online catalog and copying (or downloading) catalog information. Over 27 million records of materials in a variety of languages and formats are accessible. The Uniform Resource Location (URL) for LC is: <http://www.loc.gov>. A growing number of libraries are adding their cataloged holdings to the WWW, although their entire bibliographic records may not always be accessible. (See appendix E for a listing of library-related Internet resources.)

Levels and Types of Processing for Library Materials

As previously mentioned, most libraries either obtain their cataloging and classification information from another source, or purchase their library materials preprocessed with the catalog cards. A variety of options are available to libraries.

Book Numbers

Besides the classification, libraries often add another number immediately below the classification which is known as the *book number*. This number is a combination of first letter of the author's last name, followed by a numerical code. The purpose of this book number is to differentiate the book from others on the same subject, and to aid in shelving and retrieving the item. The most common tool which libraries use for establishing a book number is the *Cutter Table*, which is cited at the end of the chapter. There are many refinements to this, but the small library manager should not experience further need for these, unless the collection grows substantially.

Processing Kits: Many publishers and jobbers offer a processing kit which usually contains a full set of catalog cards, and may also include a spine label with the classification number, a book pocket and a book card. However, it is always wise to determine what is included in the kit, since the contents may vary. It is also important to remember that processing kits use standard cataloging and classification.

Fully Processed: Libraries can purchase books completely processed and ready for circulation from jobbers and other suppliers and cooperative processing centers. There is often some degree of flexibility in how the books are processed, since libraries use different types of circulation systems, and differ on classification systems. Jobbers and processing centers will offer a set of specifications from which the library manager can choose.

Catalog Cards: A number of organizations and firms can supply catalog card sets for a modest sum. One of the largest suppliers of catalog cards in the nation is the Online Computer Library Center (OCLC) located at 6565 Frantz Road, Dublin, OH. This is a nonprofit cooperative organization with thousands of member libraries throughout the world. They deliver their services through state, regional and international networks. In the U.S., each state library agency can furnish information on the nearest network. Libraries in other nations should contact OCLC directly (614/764-6000). Although OCLC is organized as an online service for members, a wide range of options are available, and it is possible for even the smallest library to develop a cooperative agreement with other libraries to share the costs and benefits. Catalog cards can be custom designed to the member library's specifications, and shipped in filing order.

Computerized Catalog Systems

Many suppliers offer package cataloging systems which can be installed on microcomputers, and which will generate full sets of catalog cards, or convert this information into a format for a fully computerized, or online, catalog. At one time these systems could only be purchased by larger libraries, but the costs have been reduced substantially. In considering such systems, the library manager should always require a demonstration, and ask about both the purchase and maintenance costs, as well as service in the event of problems. If the system contains cataloging and classification, it is of critical importance to determine whether that information is in a standard format (AACR2), how it is kept current, and what is the subscription cost.

If the library manager proposes to use a computerized catalog for public service (which is called a Public Access Catalog or PAC), it will be important to determine the form of entry and the search capabilities of the system, as well as capacity and growth potential. A standard format for computerized catalog information has been developed by the Library of Congress called Machine Readable Cataloging (MARC), and it is highly desirable for the system to have the capability and design to accommodate it. If it does not, the day may come when the system would have to be upgraded and all the records would have to be converted, which would be a costly and time consuming task.

Most state library agencies and cooperative systems can provide information on where full processing can be obtained. In using these services, managers should inquire on the time required for processing, in addition to cost and specifications.

Advice from The Frugal Librarian

The Frugal Librarian suggests that another option which a small library might explore is a contractual arrangement with a larger nearby library for cataloging and processing. Some cooperative library systems offer this as an option, or can provide referral to services capable of handling this work.

Search capabilities are also important. While many PACs offer the capacity to search by author, title and subject, it would be very useful if the system had the capacity for Boolean or keyword searching. *Boolean* searching allows the user to combine terms with "and", "or" or "not", while *keyword* searching allows the file to be searched literally on a word by word basis. It takes an extremely powerful system to have these capabilities, and it may not be possible for the library to purchase it. However, it would be valuable to determine whether the system has the capacity to be upgraded or expanded in the future.

The growth potential of the system is also very important, and whether it might be linked to other computers in the institution and organization, to expand access to the collection. These are questions to ask the sales representative. However, the library manager will need to provide the representative with the current size of the collection, and planned use and growth, so the system can be configured accurately. There is a tendency on the part of many sales representatives to underconfigure the system in order to quote a lower and more attractive price. This might lead the library manager to buy a system which proves too small for the future growth of the collection. If the library manager is unfamiliar with computers, it would be valuable to hire a consultant to help in developing specifications and for evaluating proposals. The state library agency or local cooperative library system can suggest qualified consultants.

Dealing with Donated Materials

Virtually every library will eventually receive an offer of donated books or other library materials, and it is desirable to have a policy on how they are to be treated. Donations can be a valuable source of materials. They can also be costly to process and catalog, and there may be strings tied to the gift which could cause problems in the future. It is recommended that all donations be accepted with the understanding that the library will use them, if they are appropriate for the collection. If not, the library will see that they are referred to another library, sold to raise funds for other purchases, donated to a charitable cause, or discarded if no other recipient can be found.

Organizing Pamphlets, Magazines and Other Print and Nonprint Materials

Pamphlets can be a valuable resource for any type of library, but they should not be cataloged or elaborately processed. It is recommended that they be placed in file folders, and that subject headings be assigned using *Sears*. There are suppliers of pressure sensitive labels containing *Sears* or other specialized subject headings developed for certain types of libraries, and they frequently advertise in the popular library publications, or library suppliers may offer these sets.

Magazines: Magazines are almost universally filed or shelved alphabetically by their title. A critical question in organizing this portion of the library's collection is the determination of how many years backfile should be retained. Records of the usage should be kept to aid in this decision. Another factor is whether another nearby library also has a file, and whether your library staff

If the library has a microcomputer, the Frugal Librarian suggests that it be used to generate labels for the pamphlet file. Many word processing software packages include label generation capability. Mailing label software is also available at low cost. Using this feature, the library staff could either develop customized subject headings for the file, or transfer subject headings from another source such as the library's automated catalog.

or its users could obtain convenient access to this collection. If backfiles are maintained, the next question is whether to bind the issues. Many library suppliers sell good quality, economical boxes in various sizes for storing back issues. Advocates of binding believe that it avoids loss, and it keeps the issues in proper order. The library manager should examine the costs and the usage, and reach a decision that is in the best interest of the library user. Newspapers may be shelved alphabetically by title or by city.

Microforms: Microforms (i.e., microfilm or microfiche) are generally filed alphabetically in order by title, similar to magazines, and chronologically under the title. Special filing cabinets are needed to properly store these resources. There is somewhat less standardization in how audiovisual materials are organized. Some libraries strongly believe in treating these materials just like books, for ease of access. They provide full cataloging, and shelf the materials or integrate them with the book collection. They argue that information on the same subject should be shelved together, regardless of the format. Other libraries believe that different formats should be shelved and cataloged or indexed separately. Their argument is that some audiovisual formats might be damaged or lost if they are on the shelf, and many users are usually looking for specific formats. Much depends on the extent of the audiovisual collection, and the patterns of the library's users. A large audiotape or compact disk collection may justify a segregated section of the library if the users find that it is easier for them to browse.

Audiovisual Materials: If the manager makes a decision to separate audiovisual materials by format, there are a number of alternatives for organizing the materials. Videotape is often shelved alphabetically by title, although some libraries assign a number, and provide access through a card or computer file. Audiocassettes, phonodisks and compact disks may be filed by artist, composer, subject or title, or a combination of these alternatives, similar to the organization of many music stores. Many libraries have developed special cataloging and classification schemes, but these are not recommended.

Government Documents: Government documents are frequently shelved according to their Superintendent of Documents (SuDocs) number. This number is cited in the *Monthly Catalog of U.S. Government Publications*, making this a convenient index to the collection. However, this becomes unwieldy if the library acquires only a few government documents. If that is the case, it is recommended that books be cataloged and shelved with the book collection, and that pamphlet type materials be placed in the vertical files.

Alternatives to Cataloging and Classification

Library managers may avoid the necessity to catalog and classify materials if there is a satisfactory alternative index or access tool, such as the *Monthly Catalog* for government documents. For example, many libraries shelve fiction in alphabetical order by the author's last name. Autobiographies and biographies can be shelved under the subject's name. Some forms of information can be filed by subject, such as pamphlets. In some instances a simple acquisition number could be assigned, and the material could be accessed by index. Audiovisual materials are more often organized in these ways because commercial cataloging is not as readily available for these resources. However, this is changing as the newer electronic formats are becoming more popular.

Weeding

One of the most difficult responsibilities the library manager will have is selecting which materials should be discarded, weeded or deaccessioned. These are used interchangeably by librarians. Few libraries have the space and equipment to keep everything they receive indefinitely. Materials become outdated, or simply wear out. Topics that were of interest five years ago are no longer pertinent. Space must be obtained for newer materials. Laws and regulations are superseded, and new research findings may make the information in scientific or medical texts inaccurate, The library's selection policy should contain a section on how long certain materials should be retained, and what types of materials should be discarded.

Historical information is an exception, and may be retained indefinitely. For example, a corporate library would be likely to preserve a copy of everything published relating to the company for future reference use.

The Frugal Librarian suggests that newspapers be retained for a specific time period and then discarded because of their lack of durability and space requirements. A microform edition can be purchased if reference requirements dictate. Many directories and almanacs are also of limited value when the new edition is released. Standing orders should be placed with the jobber or the publisher for these types of materials to save time, and the old edition should be discarded when the new edition is received.

Guidelines for Organizing the Library Collection

1 Use a standard cataloging and classification system.

2 Buy catalog kits or preprocessed materials whenever possible.

3 Computerize if the organization and use of the collection begins to occupy a significant portion of the manager's time.

4 Don't become obsessed with the organization of the collection to the extent that it interferes with service to the user.

5 Use natural order for organizing various formats in the library, such as title order for periodicals.

6 Weeding the collection is just as important as selecting new resources, if the library is to be kept current and attractive.

Resources

Abridged Dewey Decimal Classification and Relative Index, 13th ed. Dublin, OH: OCLC Forest Press, 1997. 1023p.

Anderson, Jacqulyn, editor-compiler. *How to Process Media*. Nashville, TN: Broadman, 1991.

Beall, Julianne. *Dewey for Windows Guide.* Dublin, OH: OCLC Forest Press, 1998. 212p.

Chan, Lois M. *A Guide to the Library of Congress Classification*, 5th ed. Englewood, CO: Libraries Unlimited, 1999. 551p.

Chan, Lois, et al. *Dewey Decimal Classification: A Practical Guide,* 2nd ed. Dublin, OH: OCLC Forest Press, 1992. 246p.

Curley, Arthur, and Jana Varlejs. *Akers' Simple Library Cataloging*, 7th, completely rev. ed. Metuchen, NJ: Scarecrow, 1984.

Cutter, C.A. *Cutter-Sanborn Three-figure Author Table: Swanson-Swift Revision*. Englewood, CO: Libraries Unlimited, 1969. 34p.

Davis, Sydney W., and Gregory R. New. *Abridged 13 Workbook: For Small Libraries: Using Dewey Decimal Classification Abridged Edition 13*. Dublin, OH: OCLC Forest Press, 1997. 71p.

Dewey Decimal Classification and Relative Index, 21st ed. Dublin, OH: OCLC Forest Press, 1996. 4 vols.

Dewey for Windows, ver. 2.00. Dublin, OH: OCLC Forest Press, 2000. (CD-ROM) Annual.

Evans, G. Edward, and Sandra M. Heft. *Introduction to Technical Services,* 6th ed. Englewood, CO: Libraries Unlimited, 1994. 534p.

Ferl, Terry E., and Larry Millsap. *Subject Cataloging: A How-to-Do-It Workbook for Librarians*. New York: Neal-Schuman,1991. 92p.

Fritz, Deborah A. *Cataloging with AACR2 and USMARC: For Books, Computer Files, Serials, Sound Recordings, and Videorecordings*. Chicago: ALA, 2000. 608p.

Godden, Irene P., ed. *Library Technical Services: Operations & Management*, 2nd ed. San Diego, CA: Academic Press, 1991. 284p.

Gorman, Michael. *The Concise AACR2*. Chicago: ALA, 1998. 176p.

Hoffman, Herbert H. *Small Library Cataloging*, 2nd ed. Metuchen, NJ: Scarecrow,1986. 226p.

Intner, Sheila S., and Josephine R. Fang. *Technical Services in the Medium-Sized Library*. Hamden, CT: Shoe String,1991. 194p.

Miller, Joseph, ed. *Sears List of Subject Headings*, 16th ed. New York: H.W. Wilson, 1997. 786p.

Miller, Rosalind, and Jane Terwillegar. *Commonsense Cataloging: A Cataloger's Manual*, 4th ed., rev. New York: H.W. Wilson, 1990. 182p.

Millsap, Larry, and Terry Ellen Ferl. *Descriptive Cataloging for AACR2 and the Integrated MARC Format*. rev. ed. New York: Neal-Schuman, 1997. 269p.

Price, Anne, ed. *Middle and Junior High School Library Catalog*, 7th ed. New York: H.W.Wilson, 1995. 1008p.

Public Library Catalog, 11th ed. New York: H.W. Wilson, 1999. 1456p.

Senior High School Library Catalog, 15th ed. New York: H.W. Wilson, 1997. 1400p.

Seely, Pauline A. *ALA Rules for Filing Catalog Cards*, 2nd ed., abridged. Chicago, ALA, 1968. 104p.

Slote, Stanley J. *Weeding Library Collections*, 4th ed. Englewood, CO: Libraries Unlimited, 1997. 240p.

Taylor, Arlene. *Bohdan S. Wynar's Introduction to Cataloging and Classification*, 9th ed., Englewood, CO: Libraries Unlimited, 2000. 633p.

Tracy, Joan I. *Library Automation for Library Technicians: An Introduction*. Metuchen, NJ: Scarecrow, 1986. 171p.

U.S. Library of Congress. *Subject Cataloging Division. Library of Congress Subject Headings*. Washington, DC: Library of Congress, cont.

U.S. Library of Congress. *Subject Cataloging Division. Classification: Classes A-Z*. Washington, DC: Government Printing Office, cont.

Winkel, Lois, ed. *Subject Headings for Children: A List of Subject Headings Used by the Library of Congress with Abridged Dewey Numbers Added*, 2nd ed. Dublin, OH: OCLC Forest Press, 1998. 2 vols.

Woods, William E. *Cross Reference Card System for School & Public Libraries*. Evergreen Park, IL: Woods Library Publishing, 1987.

Yaakov, Juliette, ed. *Children's Catalog*. 17th ed. New York: H.W. Wilson, 1996. 1373p.

Zuiderveld, Sharon. *Cataloging Correctly for Kids: An Introduction to the Tools*, 3rd ed. Chicago: ALA,1998. 142p.

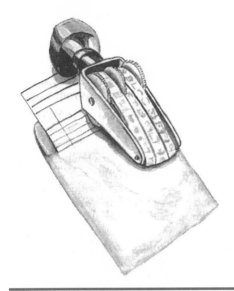

Processing and Lending Library Materials

Chapter 5

The operation of a library can be very labor intensive, requiring more time than its staff can afford. For that reason it is very important for the library manager to search for opportunities to simplify or avoid the routine or repetitive functions that have become so often associated with processing and lending library materials. Fortunately, there have been many new procedures, equipment, services and supplies that are now available to save time and money. Even greater efficiencies can be realized if the library has a microcomputer.

Preparing Books and Other Materials for Loan

There are also some principles that should be considered in establishing the library's processing and lending work. First, avoid spending more time to process and circulate library materials than they may be worth. Audiocassettes, mass market paperbacks, periodicals and pamphlets are materials which are usually ephemeral. Unless these materials are one-of-a-kind, unique to the firm or institution, or relatively costly, there is little need for full processing.

Another principle is to purchase processing kits or order the materials preprocessed whenever possible. This was mentioned in the preceding chapter. It is much more economical, and even the larger and better supported libraries use this technique because of the availability of quality cataloging today from commercial sources.

Procedures and supplies needed for preparing a book for loan will vary depending upon the type of circulation system the library uses. Typically, the steps involve:

Spine Labels: The placement of a spine label with the book's call number one inch (or whichever standard the library has adopted) from the lower edge of the book. Most publishers design their book spines to allow for this placement, particularly if the book is intended for the library market.

A good example are paperbacks. Many libraries do not catalog these materials, but simply shelve them by subject or author, particularly if they are popular fiction or children's titles. These may often just have a strip of clear plastic tape placed on the spine to strengthen the cover, and simply have the library's name and address stamped in one or more locations on the book. Certainly this would not be appropriate in a business library where the paperback is likely to be nonfiction and have reference value, but generally, paperback editions are not expected to be of a permanent nature.

Book Pockets: A book pocket is also glued on the first or last page in the book, which is usually reinforced, and a book card containing the bibliographic information and call number is inserted. Often the book pocket will contain similar information.

Date Due Slips: A due date slip may also be applied on the inside front or rear cover, to allow the due date to be stamped. Besides informing the user when the book should be returned, the date slip provides the library with indication of how often the book has been circulated. Some libraries simply stamp the due date on the inside cover of paperbacks, since they assume the book will wear out before the page is filled.

Plastic Covers: After the spine label and book pocket are inserted, many libraries apply a plastic cover to protect the book, unless the book is a paperback or hardbound edition with a printed or stamped cover. In those instances where plastic covers are not used, libraries usually place a strip of clear plastic tape over the spine label to protect it. The plastic covers come in a variety of standard sizes, as well as adjustable covers for unusual size books. These are taped onto the book.

Mark of Ownership: The library's name is then stamped or embossed in the book. Often this is rubber stamped on the fore edge, top or bottom of the book, or the title page of the book for ease in identification. Some libraries also stamp their name on a standard page inside the book to prove ownership in the event the book is stolen and the other ownership marks are sanded off. For the same reason, some libraries also emboss their name on an inside page. Unless the library experiences an unusual amount of loss, there is little need for more than two marks of ownership.

For the Computerized Collection

Libraries using an computerized circulation system do not require a book pocket or card, although they do need to have a bar code for control. These are usually scanned with a laser reader, wand or light pen. Some libraries install these bar codes on the book cover to avoid the need to open the book in the circulation process, while others install the bar code on the inside front or rear cover, since they need to open the book anyway to stamp the due date or to insert a predated due date slip. If the library uses bar codes as part of its circulation system, care should be taken in installing the bar codes. Laser readers or light pens may not be able to read bar codes which have a protective tape placed over them, or if the bar code is covered by a plastic book cover.

Filing Government Publications

If the library has extensive U.S. governmental publications, it is common to file these by their Superintendent of Documents (SuDocs No.) which can either be located on the publication or in the *Monthly Catalog*, which then serves as an index or catalog to the collection. Government documents can be economical and valuable to any type and size libraries. However, most libraries with small collections of government publications either treat them as pamphlets, and file them by subject or catalog them, and integrate them with other materials on the shelf.

Advice from the Frugal Librarian

At one time it was standard procedure to place an "acquisition" number on each book, and enter this in some other record. Few if any libraries bother with this procedure today, and the Frugal Librarian recommends there is no need to do so if the library uses bar codes, since that code becomes the unique book number for that title. As mentioned previously, materials such as pamphlets are rarely given any processing, other than a mark of ownership. Since many of these are filed by subject, some libraries may label, type or write the subject heading on the cover to ensure the item is filed correctly.

Audiovisual Materials

Processing audiovisual materials for loan is more difficult because of the variety of formats, and the fact that some materials come in kit form. A good library supply catalog will provide information on the common ways to protect and "package" these materials. The principle is to remember is to avoid spending more to protect and package these materials than they are worth. Circulation of audiovisual materials may also be specially handled because either the library may have only a limited number of these materials, or because they may be of a fragile nature. For example, videotapes and audiocassettes are protected with durable plastic cases to reduce the likelihood of damage.

Binding, Repair and Preservation

Improvements in book design and production, as well as selection of acid free paper and materials have greatly increased the durability and preservation of books during the past decade, and it can be anticipated this trend will continue as more libraries and consumers become selective in their purchasing. Whenever possible the library manager should select books using acid free or permanent paper. Many publishers prominently report their use of permanent paper in their catalogs, especially if they are interested in serving libraries. The manager should also purchase books with library bindings, wherever this is appropriate because of heavy usage. For example, children's books are especially susceptible to damage. The publisher will usually provide this information in its catalogs and advertising, but where it is not stated, the library manager should inquire. Folders, magazine files, and other materials in which permanent records and library materials are stored should also be acid free, and a good library supplier will offer these materials in its catalogs.

Nonetheless, even with these improvements, books will still be damaged and require repair. It may be possible to send these materials to a bindery, or in some instances, simple repair can be done in the library. It is always wise, however, to evaluate the item to determine whether it is worth rebinding or repair. *Books In Print* can be used to determine whether another copy can be purchased or whether a newer edition may be available. It is still cheaper to rebind many books rather than replacing them, but if the book is available in a paperback edition, it may be more economical to purchase a replacement in that format.

Not every book can be rebound. The process requires the removal of the cover and sanding the edges of the book, before a new cover is sewn or fastened in some other fashion to the book. This results in a loss of margin, particularly the inside margin or "gutter" of the book. Books which have relatively narrow margins are not good candidates. A book can be bound only a limited number of times. Moreover, the paper may have deteriorated to the extent that binding is not going to solve the problem. There are various procedures which can be used even with books which have seriously deteriorated, such as fine binding where slipcases are constructed to hold the case, or the book could be deacidified through a chemical process. However, these are expensive alternatives, and usually employed only for rare materials.

Certified library binderies advertise in library publications, and exhibit at professional conferences. State library agencies and larger libraries can provide references. These binderies use recommended techniques and materials, and they can aid in assessing whether materials can be rebound. Many libraries also bind periodical backfiles for future reference use. The library manager should carefully compare this to the purchase of microforms. Many periodicals are available in either microfilm rolls or microfiche sheets. Microform materials do not require as much shelf space, which is an important factor in a library which may have need for retaining periodical backfiles. However, they do require special microfilm or microfiche readers and printers, and these also require space. Another factor is the preference of the library users. Many persons do not like to use microform.

There are minor repairs that any library can make to save damaged

library binding: a book with reinforced end signatures, strong endpapers, stitched signatures and heavier cloth covers. Standards for "library binding" are established by the Library Binding Institute and the American Library Association. (Often there is no visual difference between a book with library binding and the regular trade edition.)

books. A good library supply catalog will contain book tape in various colors and widths to use in repairing a broken corner or to reinforce a torn cover. Clear special tape that does not contain chemicals that deteriorate paper can be purchased to mend torn pages. Reference books which have missing pages can be repaired by photocopying the missing page from a copy located in another library, and tipping or taping it in place. Libraries occasionally lose single volumes from reference sets such as encyclopedias. When this occurs, the library should always contact the publisher, who may be able to furnish a replacement volume at a reasonable cost.

A handbook describing simple repair procedures is listed at the end of this chapter. Another alternative would be to visit an older library, and to gain some instruction on simple book repair from the staff member who is responsible for this work. Library associations sponsor workshops on this at regular intervals.

Circulation Systems and Procedures

Circulation procedures are merely a means of keeping track of where materials are, who borrowed an item, and when it is due to be returned to the library. Many small libraries do not even bother with a system, particularly if access to the library is controlled and the number of users is relatively small. This is true with many business libraries. Of course, if the collection is entirely for reference use, and few materials are loaned, there is no need for any elaborate system. Nonetheless, most libraries do have some formal circulation or lending procedure, primarily because it allows the staff to know where materials are, and to better evaluate usage. There are essentially only two types of circulation systems: *manual* and *automated*.

Manual Systems

Manual systems rely upon filing procedures, transaction records, photocharging or some combinations of two or three. The most common manual procedure is the *book card system.* A card containing the book's author, title and call number is removed from the book, the borrower signs it, and it is then filed in call number order in a card tray under the due date of the book. Staff rubber stamp the due date in the book. When the book is returned, the book card is located under the appropriate due date. Books that are overdue can then be easily located, and the borrowers notified. It is relatively simple and economical, but if a specific book needs to be located, the entire file must be searched. Moreover, the system does not automatically provide statistics on the use of materials, and if a card is misfiled, the entire file must be searched. Nonetheless, for a small library that does not have a large circulation, it is a good alternative. Most library suppliers sell all the equipment that is required.

Transaction circulation systems require the completion of a slip containing the borrower's name and location. The slip is prenumbered, and there is a slip with a matching number on which the due date can be stamped which is inserted in the book pocket. When the book is returned, the numbered slip is removed, and the number is crossed off a sheet containing a complete sequence of the numbers by date. After the due date is reached, those numbers which have not been crossed off represent overdue books. The library staff can then locate the slip which was filed in numerical order, and identify and notify the overdue borrower. Again, this is a relatively simple and economical system, but it cannot determine where the books can be located at any specific point in time, nor can it provide detailed statistics on usage, other than total circulation. If the transaction slip is lost, there will also be a problem in determining when it was due. There are various systems which have refinements to get around these limitations, but they are more costly.

A *photocharge system* also uses transaction slips. A small microphoto camera is used to photograph the book and the borrower's identification card in transaction number order. The transaction card with the overdue date is inserted in the book. When the book is returned, the transaction number is crossed off the tally sheet for that date. Numbers which are not crossed off represent overdue books, and the microfilm is consulted to identify and notify the borrower. This has the same advantages and disadvantages as the preceding system, and relatively few libraries use photocharge systems today because of the difficulty of finding and maintaining the equipment.

Automated Systems

Automated systems may use microcomputers, minicomputers or mainframe computers to keep track of circulation, and there are many commercially available systems designed for all sizes and types of libraries, from the very smallest one person library to the largest library in the nation. Some libraries in organizations that have computer service departments have developed their own computer software programs. While this offers the advantage of a custom designed system certain to operate on the organization's computer, it is recommended that a software package be purchased, especially for a small library, since the cost is likely to be less that the development and testing time for new software, and because the packages which are now available have been widely tested and applied in many different libraries. *Why reinvent the wheel!*

Circulation system software is widely advertised in library publications, and virtually every library conference will have exhibitors who sell and maintain these systems. Selecting the system which is best for your library should be done in the same fashion as any other major purchase. The manager should study the literature on library computer systems to understand the features that are desirable, visit other libraries of a similar size that have automated circulation systems to benefit from their experience, and then develop specifications that describe what the system must handle at the present time, in terms of borrowers, circulation, library holdings, and projected future growth for the next five years. If the library manager does not feel comfortable developing these specifications and evaluating proposals, a consultant should be retained. The cooperative library system, state library agency or a nearby larger library can provide lists of qualified automation consultants.

There are two factors that must be considered in the purchase of an automated circulation system. One is the cost and time required for conversion to the system. The second is the maintenance and reliability of the system. The *conversion process* involves bar coding all the library's holdings, building a database containing the bibliographic records for each of the items in the collection that will be circulated through the system, and building a database of borrower names and locations. With a new library, this

Why select a computerized system?

Despite its greater initial cost and the steps required to convert to the system, in the long term it is the best way for the library manager to control the collection, serve the library's users, and plan for the future. Virtually every small library should consider an automated circulation system, because it will save staff time, and that is the greatest expense the library will have, both in the present and in the future. A variety of circulation systems are available for small libraries. They can be installed on microcomputers, and if the equipment is purchased with sufficient storage capacity and speed, the same microcomputer can also be used to handle other library applications.

information can be assembled as the collection is developed. With an established library, a ***retrospective conversion*** of these records must take place. Maintenance is very important for a computerized system because the library will be making a long term commitment to that system. The library manager must be certain that the firm that sells the system will have the capability both now and in the future to service the system, provide training, and have personnel capable of resolving future problems.

Library Borrowers Cards

Because almost everyone has owned a library card at some time in their life, the library manager will eventually be faced with question of whether the library should issue cards. The answer is that they are needed only if the usage is not controlled. In a small business or church, for example, where access is limited to only a few hundred persons or members of the congregation, and where the library staff know all users, the issuance of a card is another clerical routine that can be avoided. However, if the users are varied, and they may not be known by the staff, some identification is essential.

Circulation Procedures

Every library needs a written set of circulation procedures to aid in training, and to ensure consistency in practice. Typically these procedures include loan periods, borrower eligibility, overdue notification, fees and fines, limitations on the number of items loaned, replacement and damage charges, and the myriad other details associated with library operation. For some small libraries where the usage is low and access to the collection is controlled, such as a business or legal library, these policies are likely to be relatively brief, and flexibly interpreted. In a busy small school library, these may have more importance, since the policies may be designed to prepare students to use larger public and college libraries. There are several good circulation manuals listed in the bibliography at the end of this chapter that can be consulted to provide a basis for a variety of libraries. Another alternative is to contact another library of the same size and type, and ask to borrow their circulation policies. Whatever the source, the library's advisory committee or a group of the library's users should be consulted to gain their suggestions and reaction to the proposed policies before they are implemented. It is also advisable to prepare a simple brochure summarizing the most significant policies, such as loan period, renewal, overdue and damage, as well as hours of service, and to give this to new borrowers for their reference.

Overdue Fines

There is such a strong mythology regarding library overdue fines that almost every library manager will feel compelled to consider whether they should be imposed. The rationale behind overdue fines is that it provides an incentive for borrowers to return materials before they become overdue. In some situations, such as small public libraries, the fine is theoretically charged to cover the cost of notifying the delinquent borrower. In practice, relatively few special libraries impose fines. More libraries question whether overdue fines are

Rather than paying a printer for reproduction of a brochure on the library, the Frugal Librarian suggests that the Library Manager contact a local business, such as a bank, and ask them to underwrite the cost, in return for an acknowledgment on the back of the brochure. Many businesses would respond positively, and the good will that is generated may lead to larger donations in the future.

effective as an incentive, and in some cases, the administration of overdue fines costs more than is actually generated.

Supplies

As this chapter reveals, the types of supplies a library needs to purchase and stock for processing and lending materials will vary considerably, depending on the type of circulation system used, and the types of materials contained in the library's collection. Nonetheless, the following are the basic elements of a small library's supply cabinet:

Processing

> Plastic book covers (standard and adjustable)
> Library tape (clear and repair tape in various colors and widths)
> Self adhesive labels (various standard sizes)
> Book cards and pockets
> Due date slips
> Plastic cases for the types of audiovisual materials contained in the library

Circulation

> Due date stamps and pads
> Overdue or reminder notices

Resources

The following titles can be consulted to provide additional information on processing and lending library resources.

Boss, Richard. *The Library Administrator's Automation Handbook.* Information Today, 1997. 226p.

Cockerell, D. *Bookbinding & the Care of Books.* New York: Lyons & Burford, 1991.

Intner, Sheila S. *Circulation Policy in Academic, Public & School Libraries.* Westport, CT: Greenwood, 1987. 237p.

Lavender, Kenneth and Stockton, Scott. *Book Repair: A How-to-Do-It Manual for Librarians.* New York: Neal-Schuman, 1992. 150p.

Schechter, Abraham A. *Basic Book Repair Methods.* Englewood, CO: Libraries Unlimited, 1999. 102p.

Simpson, Floyd, and Glynn Hill, eds. *How to Repair Books & Maintain Audiovisuals.* Nashville, TN: Broadman, 1991.

Swan, James. *Automating Small Libraries.* Ft. Atkinson: WI: Highsmith Press, 1996. 88p.

Advice from The Frugal Librarian

To avoid running of out critical processing or circulation supplies you may want to consider an inventory control service with one of the major library supply companies below. Based on your average order size and frequency, these regular shipments can be a real time saver.

Library Suppliers

The following is a selective list of firms that sell a variety of supplies and equipment for libraries. A more comprehensive listing can be found in the *Librarian's Yellow Pages* (PO Box 179, Larchmont, NY 10538, 800/235-9723) or in the annual buyer's guide published by *Library Journal.*

Brodart
1609 Memorial Avenue
Williamsport, PA 17705
Tel. 888/820-4377
Web: www.brodart-sf.com

Demco
PO Box 7488
Madison, WI 53707
Tel. 800/356-1200
Fax: 800/245-1329
Web: www.demco.com

Gaylord Bros.
Box 4901
Syracuse, NY 13221-4901
Tel. 800/448-6160
Fax: 800/272-3412
Web: www.gaylord.com

Highsmith Inc.
PO Box 800
Ft. Atkinson, WI 53538-0800
Tel. 800/558-2110
Fax: 800/835-2329
E-mail: service@highsmith.com
Web: www.highsmith.com

Designing the Efficient and Attractive Library

Chapter 6

Libraries should be designed for the convenience of both users and staff. They need to be attractive, easy to use, and offer sufficient display and storage space for resources. Unfortunately, many library managers are limited by cost and space constraints in designing their facilities. Often they are assigned a specific area and budget, and directed to make the best of it. While funding and space assignments cannot be ignored, if the library is not both *attractive* and *efficient*, the organization will not derive real benefits from the facility. It will either not attract usage, or it will be more costly to operate and maintain.

Individuals often have a preconception of what a library should be based on what they remember of a favorite school, public or college library. Any library manager with the responsibility for establishing a new facility or remodeling an existing library should avoid that pitfall, and begin her planning based on user needs and work requirements. For example, many small libraries may not require a card catalog or circulation desk. Book shelving may be inappropriate for certain types of special libraries.

The Program

It is often tempting to begin sketching a floor plan as the first step in designing any space. Unfortunately, important requirements can be omitted, and for that reason it is recommended that every library manager prepare a document called a ***building program***. Taking the time to develop a written program can provide the manager and those who will assist her in the design with a checklist that can improve the efficiency and aesthetic appearance of the library, making it more attractive to users. Using this building program and preliminary space estimates, plans can be developed to either reallocate existing space more effectively, or to provide guidance to an architect or space designer in constructing or developing a new library.

A library building program contains the following basic elements:

Public Services: Determine how much seating is needed or desirable, and

library building program: written description of the various functional requirements of the library, including public services, collection and work space requirements.

should this be provided in the form of tables and chairs, or would individual study carrels be more appropriate for the users. What sort of special equipment will the users need, such microfilm readers or photocopy machines? Is a desk needed by the staff to serve the users? What sort of lighting and electrical power will be required? If conference rooms are needed, the number and seating requirements need to be determined. All of this information can be used to estimate the amount of square footage required. For example, space planners generally estimate five sq. ft. is required for every reader station, but the library manager can develop her own measurements if special requirements dictate.

Collection: Describe the types of materials the library will collect, and estimate the initial size of this collection, and the projected growth five to twenty years in the future. If special storage requirements exist, such as locked cases for rare or expensive materials, this should be stated in the program. The height of the shelving should also be stated. By using the standard measurements in the side-bar, the library manager can arrive at a suitable formula for the amount of floor space required for the collection.

Work Space: Determine the amount of office, work or other special requirements needed. An individual office generally requires 150 sq. ft., but more or less space may be required depending on the work that individual performs, and the special equipment required. Certain functions that generate noise may require privacy to avoid interference with library use. The library manager should also plan to provide work areas with good lighting and sufficient telephone and electrical outlets, as well as generous storage space to avoid clutter.

If the library manager does not have an architect or space designer to assist her, the building program can be used to prepare a simple floor plan, which would be the next step in the design process. Plastic templates for this purpose can be found in many library supply catalogs or purchased from larger office outfitters. Simple computer software is also available for this purpose. Generally a floor plan is drawn to a scale where $^1/4$" equals one foot, but this will depend on the size of the library space.

It is also recommended that other libraries be visited to gain ideas on attractive and efficient layout and equipment, and insight on how problems were solved. Sometimes, errors and omissions can be observed or learned from the library's staff. For example, a high degree of clutter may reveal a lack of adequate storage space. Consultants may be helpful in planning more efficient space, and a current list can be located in *The Librarian's Yellow Pages* (also available on the Internet [Telnet–database.carl.org]) or in the annual buying guide published by *Library Journal.* If funds permit, it is recommended that this expert assistance be sought. Certain architectural firms specialize in library design. Some librarians who have designed several libraries are available for consultant assistance. Interior designers can identify equipment, colors, textures and other elements that will make the library more attractive and efficient. Generally architects and consultants such as interior designers are paid based on a percentage of the total project cost, but it may be possible to negotiate other terms such as hourly rates or lump sum payment. The state library agency or cooperative library system serving your area may be

Standard Library Shelving Measurements

Heights
Children's Shelving: 48"
Reference Shelving: 48"
Intermediate Shel.: 60"
Standard Shelving: 82"

Standard Width: 36"

Depths: 8", 10" and 12"

Materials: metal or wood

Facing: Double or Single

To estimate space: A standard height, single-faced section of shelving will accommodate 250 books, but this will vary depending on the nature of the collection.

(It is possible to order special heights, widths and depths at greater cost.)

able to provide a listing of building consultants, architects and designers who have experience in library building projects.

Furnishings

While equipment such as shelving, tables and chairs can be purchased from office supply firms and other commercial sources, it is strongly recommended that equipment be selected that is designed to meet library standards. Tables, chairs and other technical equipment designed for libraries have a legendary durability, and many firms specializing in the library market now offer a wide range of attractive styles appropriate for your facility. These firms advertise in library publications and exhibit at library conferences. Many library suppliers also include these products in their catalogs. While some libraries like the convenience of purchasing their equipment from a local office furnishing store or a discount outlet, they should examine equipment designed to meet library standards before a purchasing decision is reached. A decision based solely on price may result in using equipment that lacks the strength and durability required by the library.

The common sizes of library shelving was mentioned earlier. In addition, it is important to ensure that library standard shelving is used for reasons of safety and durability. All quality shelving is braced to avoid collapse, and special anti-sway bracing is mandatory in areas prone to earthquakes. Single-face shelving is generally called perimeter or wall shelving, and it needs to be securely anchored to the walls to avoid collapse.

Lounge furniture or informal seating is often used to contribute to the aesthetic appearance, but care should be taken that it will stand up to the traffic. Hotel quality sofas and lounge chairs are selected by many libraries, despite their extra cost, because of the longer life and durability.

Special or technical equipment such as atlas cases, dictionary stands, card catalogs, are usually the most costly elements of library furnishings, and care will be needed in specifying how many of these items should be included in the library's design. In selecting tables and study carrels, care should be taken in specifying surfaces which can be easily maintained. Wood may be perfectly satisfactory in a corporate or law library, where good custodial care is available and vandalism is unlikely, but a formica top may be more practical in a school library.

Audiovisual equipment imposes additional requirements. It is very common today for libraries to have microforms, film, videotape, audiotape, CD-ROMs, and a variety of other formats. It is a rule that if the library stocks these formats, it should provide the equipment to allow the user to have access. That necessitates special planning requirements, such as additional electrical outlets. Projection equipment such as microform readers require darkened spaces, and sound proofing in some instances. Video and audio tape players will require carrels and headsets. Telephone or computer cable outlets also need to be planned, and if a new facility is being designed, the library manager must inform the architect or designer of this possibility so that conduit is installed to accommodate this need. Otherwise some expensive remodeling may be required in the future, or unsightly exterior molding may have to be used.

If the library collects maps, pamphlets, magazines, government docu-

Furnishings Checklist

Work space seating
Shelving
Lounge furniture
Special or technical equipment
Audiovisual equipment
Filing cabinets, special storage
Photocopiers

Internet Considerations

Libraries of all types and sizes are adding computer stations to permit users access to Internet resources. Following are some suggestions for planning and selection of equipment offered by Andrea Johnson, Marketing Director for Texwood, Inc.

Plan for a larger ratio of sit-down stations, plus some stand-up and wheelchair accessible ones, or—purchase adjustable-height stations.

Choose a workstation that has a large grommet or channel on the work surface for wire management. Also, determine where your outlets will be relative to under-surface channels. Look for the ability to connect data and electrical wires through under-surface channels between workstations to the floor or wall outlets.

The size and style of computer hardware plays a big role in the selection of workstations and circulation desks. It is very important to measure both the CPU and the depth of the computer monitor before selecting furniture.

Plan to purchase some library tables with electrical and telephone jacks on the work surface for laptop users.

Select modular circulation desks that allow sufficient room and flexibility for self-check systems, scanners, desensitizers, computers, and printers. Don't forget to plan for an ADA-height module for patrons with disabilities.

ments, photographs, and other unusual formats, it may also require filing cabinets or vertical files, as they are called in libraries. It is always recommended that good quality files be selected because of their durability and safety. Plan to add special equipment whenever new formats are added to the library's collection.

Photocopiers are now a fundamental piece of equipment for all types and sizes of libraries. Plain paper copiers are essential. Have a service agreement with the leasor or seller, because the equipment is prone to breakdown, no matter what the salesperson claims.

Environmental Concerns

Proper lighting is very important in every library. Some natural light is always desirable for aesthetic purposes, but it might create glare and heat problems if it is excessive, or if the library houses sensitive or rare materials easily damaged by the sun. Draperies, blinds, shades or other window treatments would be an important consideration if the library does have windows that admit extensive light. Artificial lighting should be adequate to avoid dark spots, and an architect or lighting consultant can advise as to the level of lighting (usually measured in foot candles), and the type of lighting that is best. At one time 100 foot candles was recommended for library lighting, but many now recommend a lower level because of improvements in design, and a greater awareness of the contribution of excessive light levels to eye strain.

Care should be taken in the design of the library's heating, ventilating and air conditioning (HVAC) system. Excess humidity or a lack of humidity can destroy the book collection, and extremes in heat and cold will certainly influence library usage. It is also important to control noise. The HVAC system should be designed to avoid annoying sound, and many libraries are carpeted today to reduce the impact of normal conversation, moving chairs an other ambient sounds. Office landscaping that employs acoustical panels which absorb sound is another option to consider, and it offers flexibility in layout as library space requirements evolve.

Selection and Purchase of Library Equipment

The library manager should gain experience in the development of specifications whenever equipment is purchased. There are two types of specifications. *Functional specifications* are those which contain a description of the equipment and its function. These are often technical in nature and the library manager may need specialized assistance in drafting the requirements. *Comparative specifications* will identify a piece of equipment by manufacturer, model and style, and indicate that this product "or equal" is desired. Consultants can be retained to assist in the development of either type of specification, but even in these instances, the library manager must give careful guidance to ensure that the right equipment is ordered. It is also highly desirable to follow the principle of requiring a minimum of three quotations to ensure that the best price is obtained. Use reliable suppliers or manufacturers, and always inquire regarding their warranty or return policy.

Access

The Americans with Disabilities Act (ADA) now requires virtually all libraries to be accessible to persons with disabilities. This means that a person in a wheelchair should be able to gain access to the library and its collections. Facilities such as restrooms and equipment such as computer terminals may need modification to provide reasonable access. Even library tables may need to be raised to allow an individual using a wheelchair to gain access. There are references at the end of the chapter on the ADA and its requirements, and it is strongly recommended that the library manager familiarize herself with the provisions of the Act, and the compliance requirements.

Advice from The Frugal Librarian

Attendance at library conferences can result in some savings on library furniture and equipment. The Frugal Librarian suggests that vendors who display new furnishings and equipment at these shows be asked whether they will sell their samples at a discount. Many will offer substantial discounts and arrange for packing and delivery. If they are displaying equipment the library manager needs, great savings can be realized. Don't forget to bring a purchase order!

Selection of Architects and Consultants

Using the list of architects or consultants collected during library visits and conferences or provided by the state library agency or cooperative library system, prepare a written specification or description of the work that is needed for distribution to them. Attach the building program. Identify any special requirements such as deadlines, cost restrictions, minimum qualifications. Ask for a written proposal and detailed cost estimate, including expenses and other miscellaneous charges. Require a list of clients. Ask them to identify any exception to your requirements, and specify when they can start. Also note that you reserve the right to reject any and all proposals and waive any irregularities. If possible, identify the criteria you will be using in selecting an architect or consultant, and where the heaviest weight will be given, such as experience or cost.

Fair evaluation and selection of these professionals, and negotiation of reasonable terms will require some insight into current practices in the building industry. Several titles listed in the resources at the end of this chapter will be helpful, but *Designing Better Libraries: Selecting and Working With Building Professionals* by Richard McCarthy, is especially recommended.

Maintenance

Probably the most important element in having an attractive and efficient library is maintenance. No one enjoys using or working in a facility that is dirty, cluttered or run down. If the library is not part of an institution that provides maintenance and custodial service, it would be advisable to consider contracting with a commercial firm for this service. This avoids problems with scheduling and reduces supervisory responsibility. The service provides the cleaning and maintenance or does not get paid. Again, specifications need to be written to define the work that needs to be performed.

Library shelving needs to be regularly dusted. There are also manufacturer's instructions for maintaining most surfaces, and many libraries experience premature aging or serious damage when carpeting, tile floors, tables and counters are not cleaned in accordance with those instructions, using harsh chemicals or abrasive cleaners. The specifications also need to define which forms of maintenance will be conducted by the service, such as light bulb replacement, lawn care (if appropriate), snow removal, and similar issues. If the custodian is an employee, and the library manager is responsible for supervising that individual, a job description defining duties and responsibilities should be written and regularly reviewed with the individual, and a schedule of major routines such as frequency of floor waxing should be prepared. See chapter 10 on the development of a job description.

Protecting the Library

The library manager needs to know the library's insurance coverage. Frequently the library is covered under a blanket policy purchased by the parent organization. However, there are special insurance policies designed for protecting libraries and their contents. The library manager should ask the institution's agent to compare one of these with the standard package they have

Electronic Islands

Richard McCarthy, AIA, of Burnidge Cassell Associates, offers the following advice on meeting the special challenges of adding computers to smaller spaces.

Consider including one or more "electronic islands" in your desgin. These are areas that meet the special requirements of computer usage. Following are useful features to consider:

A lower ceiling plane. Many libraries have high ceilings to allow the use of indirect lighting fixtures, along with windows that are either floor to ceiling or placed near the ceiling. A lower ceiling in the computer area will reduce the amount of glare from high windows in adjacent spaces.

Low surface-brightness direct lighting fixtures. Using these fixtures in place of indirect fixtures will darken the ceiling plane and further help to eliminate glare.

Extensive pre-wiring of the electronic island. Pre-wiring designated electronic islands is less expensive than attempting to pre-wire an entire building to allow computers to be placed anywhere.

Sound-absorbing materials. Adding these materials around computer areas will reduce the amount of distraction caused by printers and other noisy peripherals.

Distinctive appearance. This will serve as an architectural signpost that tells patrons where to find the computers.

Staffing efficiency. Strategic placement of electronic islands near staff service points reduces the amount of time required to assist patrons.

for the parent organization. Libraries have many unique hazards and features, such as the value of the collection, which may not be considered in the organization's policy. If there is no parent organization, and the library is not protected by insurance, the library manager should seek to correct this omission.

When discussing insurance coverage with an agent, the library manager should make certain that the extent of coverage is based on replacement cost rather than original cost. If this is not the basis for claim settlement, and a loss occurs, the library may not receive sufficient funds to replace the facility, equipment and collection. Insurance firms also require some inventory record, to serve as a basis for coverage. Generally this is handled by an annual update consisting of the types of resources, their numbers, and an inventory of the physical equipment located in the library. However, the manager should remember that certain records cannot be replaced, even if they are insured, such as the bibliographic records of the library. If the library is computerized, a copy of these records should be regularly made and stored somewhere other than in the same building.

Conclusion

Invest in cleanliness and attractive design. It will ensure that the facility is used. Insist on functional and efficient design to avoid extra time and lost energy. Require library standard quality furnishings and equipment for safety and durability. Be creative in displaying the library's resources to add color and variety to the area.

Resources

The following materials will be of further value in designing the most efficient and attractive library to satisfy the requirements of users.

Alire, Camila, ed. ***Library Disaster Planning and Recovery Handbook.*** New York: Neal-Schuman, 2000. 500p.

American Library Trustees Association. ***Determining Your Public Library's Future Size: A Needs Assessment & Planning Model.*** Chicago: ALA, 1996. 155p.

Brown, Carol R. ***Planning Library Interiors: The Selection of Furnishings for the 21st Century.*** 2nd ed. Phoenix, AZ: Oryx Press, 1995. 168p.

Dahlgren, Anders C. ***Planning the Small Public Library Building.*** Chicago: ALA, 1996. 40p.

————. ***Wisconsin Library Building Project Handbook,*** rev. ed. Madison, WI: Wisconsin Department of Public Instruction, 1991. 219p.

Feinberg, Sandra, et al. ***Learning Environments for Young Children: Rethinking Library Spaces & Services.*** Chicago: ALA, 1998. 196p.

Holt, Raymond M. ***Planning Library Buildings & Facilities (From Concept to Completion).*** Metuchen, NJ: Scarecrow, 1989. 260p.

Kahn, Miriam B. ***Disaster Response and Planning for Libraries.*** Chicago: ALA, 1998. 144p.

Koontz, Christine. ***Library Facility Siting & Location Handbook.*** Westport, CT: Greenwood, 1997. 224p.

McCarthy, Richard. ***Designing Better Libraries: Selecting & Working with Building Professionals.*** 2nd ed. Ft. Atkinson, WI: Highsmith Press, 1999. 132p.

Mount, Ellis. ***Creative Planning of Special Library Facilities.*** Binghamton, NY: Haworth Press, 1988. 197p.

Advice from The Frugal Librarian

To establish an insured value for the collection, some libraries will hire a qualified appraiser. While expert advice is always desirable, the Frugal Librarian suggests another alternative if funds are limited. Both *Publishers Weekly* and the *Bowker Annual* regularly list the average cost of newly published books in many different categories, such as children's titles. Using these average prices, and multiplying by the estimated or actual number of books in each category, a total retail value for the collection can be determined. Multiplying that figure by the library's average discount will produce the current replacement value for the collection.

More Like a Bookstore

Many libraries are being influenced by bookstore design. Shelving in a bookstore makes browsing easier by pointing book spines and covers upward towards customers. The bottom shelf is tipped upward and outward, creating a triangular shape that is wider at the bottom and narrower at the top. The shelving in the middle of the room is under 60" in height. This allows more light into the room and makes it easier to monitor spaces.

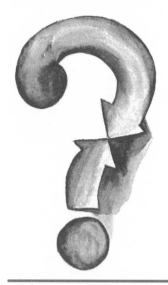

Reference and Information Services

Chapter 7

Responding promptly and accurately to user requests for information is one of the primary functions of a library. However, libraries differ considerably in how they treat these requests, and in their capability to respond. School libraries, for example, need to educate students to learn research procedures and common reference books. The staff in these libraries will not necessarily provide the answer to the question that student may have, but they may devote considerable effort to teaching the student how to use different resources to find that answer. Legal, medical or corporate libraries, on the other hand, may conduct exhaustive research for their clientele. Advanced training may be required for library personnel serving professional personnel to be familiar with the terminology of the field and specialized resource tools. Therefore, it is very important that the library have policies regarding the nature and extent of reference services to be extended to users, and these policies need to be determined at the outset.

There are several alternatives the manager can take in defining or developing these policies. For example, the library's advisory committee, composed of users, or the executive who supervises the library manager can certainly provide input on their expectations. Contacts with similar small libraries can determine their practices. Some of the texts dealing with special types of libraries, which are cited under the later chapters in this book can provide guidance. If extensive reference service is expected or is customary, the library's staff must have the qualifications, either in terms of formal training or experience, to handle this responsibility. If they do not have this experience or training, the organization must be prepared to invest in training the library's staff involved in this work. Another alternative would be to contract for special reference services, or to be able to refer users to larger or more specialized libraries. More libraries are willing to extend such service, and this should be explored with appropriate institutions in the area.

Reference Interview

Even if the staff has the technical knowledge or is able to refer questions to other libraries, it is necessary for the library manager and any staff member who may become associated with the reference and referral process to know how to conduct a reference interview. Studies have shown that many individuals do not know how to articulate information questions because they are either not certain of what information they are seeking, or they are unaware of what resources are available to aid them. The library staff must be the navigator, and avoid making assumptions based on what they believe the user is seeking.

Great sensitivity and care must be taken to ensure that the user does not infer that you are prying, or that their question is frivolous or unimportant. First of all, the interview should be conducted as privately as possible. That may be difficult if the library is busy, and others are waiting for service, but every effort should be made to make the individual comfortable in discussing his or her question. Notes should be taken, and the individual's telephone number or location should be obtained for follow-up or further clarification. If possible, some insight should be obtained as to how the information is to be used, or the context in which the question arose. Determine whether there are any parameters that will allow the search to be focused to a specific time, location, or subject. If specialized terms or names are part of this question, make certain to ask for their correct spelling, Above all, ask the person's advice on sources that may be of help. They may have undertaken some preliminary research that will avoid the necessity of checking certain resources.

... o another library, make certain to provide all ... name and telephone number so they can ... y. Follow-up with the user to ensure their ... ly.

... tion is obtained from the library's collec- ... ld be informed of the source. This will ... er or to gain further clarification if nec- ... vidual in the future, since it may allow ... in the event library staff is occupied ... dds credibility to the answer when a

... hotocopy information from a refer- ... nd to the user's reference question. ... copyright restrictions in the repro- duction of information. Virtually all commercially produced material is copyrighted, either by the publisher, producer or the author, in order to protect this intellectual property. Many educational institutions, nonprofit organizations, and even some governmental agencies copyright their publications. Any material that bears a copyright symbol or states it is copyrighted is protected by federal law in the United States, and by international treaty agreement throughout most of the world. Individuals and institutions are subject to a lawsuit if they reproduce copyrighted material improperly, and this applies to nonprofit organizations, educational institutions, charitable

What if staff can't answer the question?

There will be no negative reflection on the library or its staff if a reference question cannot be answered, and must be referred to another source. Even the very largest libraries cannot satisfy every question they receive. Small libraries may lack the resources to answer difficult questions, and this is particularly true if the question is technical or highly specialized. However, it is always wrong to guess at an answer, and to fail to refer the question to another appropriate source, if one exists. Inaccurate reference assistance or inadequate referral practices will undermine confidence in the library.

Advice from The Frugal Librarian

Libraries often need permission to make multiple copies of copyrighted materials for their users, especially school libraries. The Frugal Librarian recommends that the following be included in the letter requesting permission:

1. The complete bibliographic description of the material to be reproduced, including the specific pages.

2. The purpose for which the material will be used, and when it will be used.

3. The number of copies to be made.

4. The requestor's name, address, telephone number, and fax and e-mail address, if available.

This information will allow the copyright holder to respond sooner, saving considerable time.

groups, and churches as well as profit-making firms.

What Does Fair Use Cover?

Copyright regulations and legal opinions have resulted in a cloudy definition of what constitutes *"fair use,"* or the circumstances under which copyrighted material may be reproduced. For example, one reproduction of a single magazine article by a student or teacher is considered fair use. On the other hand, the reproduction of 100 copies of a copyrighted hymn by a church choir director would not be fair use. This is a complicated legal issue, and the definition of what constitutes "fair use" continues to evolve. A resource is cited at the end of this chapter, but the reader is advised to keep current with the literature and more recent legal opinions. It is also recommended that the library manager consult with her parent organization's legal counsel, and gain professional advice relative to photocopying policies, as well as reproduction of other copyrighted material. Even if the user does the photocopying, the library and its parent organization assumes some liability in copyright infringement.

Selection

The leading reference selection tools are the *Guide to Reference Books*, edited by Eugene Sheehy (10th ed., Chicago, American Library Association, 1986, and the *Walford Guide to Reference Material* (3 vols., London, Library Association Publishing, 1989–92). These contain descriptive annotations to major reference tools of value to different types and sizes of libraries, and they can be examined at a larger library. Development of a library's reference collection depends to a considerable degree on its mission and clientele. However, all libraries need a basic set of standard reference tools, no matter what their clientele is or the purpose of the library. These include a careful selection of dictionaries, encyclopedias, almanacs, indexes and directories. A number of books have been published which identify basic reference collections for small libraries, and several library journals feature articles identifying the best new reference titles. These should be consulted in the development of an initial order. A good alternative is to visit another small library and examine the titles they have selected, and to ask their staff about the materials they use most frequently.

Specialized bibliographies or guides to the literature have been developed for many fields, and Sheehy and Walford can be consulted to select the more advanced tools required by special libraries. It is also important to seek the recommendations from specialists in the organization who know the field. Reference tools should be separate from the rest of the collection, since these tools do not generally circulate. The users of the reference collection also need access to a photocopier for reproducing information from the resources.

Encyclopedias

Every small library should own a current encyclopedia. Encyclopedias may be single and multivolume in length, and they may be general or special in scope. Many of the encyclopedias exercise what is known as continuous revision, i.e., they selectively revise articles annually. This means that the edition

---

Copyright Clearance Center

The publishing industry has established a clearinghouse called the Copyright Clearance Center (CCC), which is designed to grant organizations and individuals permission to reproduce copyrighted materials.

The Center is equipped to advise users the extent of photocopying allowed, and to cite the costs. Accounts can be established for the convenience of users, and this should be considered if the library does extensive photocopying.

Unfortunately, not all publishers participate in the CCC, and not all materials which are copyrighted are handled by the CCC. The safest recourse is to contact the individual or firm identified in the material as the copyright holder, and to ask their permission for reproduction. This is the name following the copyright symbol. If it is a name without an address, contact the publisher or producer for assistance. *Literary Marketplace* contains a comprehensive listing of the addresses and telephone numbers of most major publishers.

Copyright Clearance Center
27 Congress Street
Salem, MA 01970

purchased in the current year will have some articles which were entirely rewritten since the previous year, and some articles which may have had little or no revision, depending on the editors' policies or assessment of need. Signed articles are valuable because it is possible to determine the source and the qualifications of the author. Sometimes only the initials of the contributors are used, and it is necessary to refer to a listing elsewhere in the book. Encyclopedia articles are rarely dated, but the edition will provide evidence as to when it was written, unless the publication is under continuous revision. Plan to replace encyclopedias at regular intervals. Ken Kister evaluates many of the general and some of the specialized encyclopedias, and his selection guide is listed at the end of this chapter. *Booklist* also contains a Reference Book Bulletin section, which is a valuable resource for selection of all types of reference books.

Advice from The Frugal Librarian

The Frugal Librarian suggests that libraries that own multiple general purpose encyclopedias stagger replacement so they always have a current set available. Furthermore, many publishers keep back files of their multivolume general encyclopedia sets, so that lost volumes can be ordered.

Almanacs

Almanacs are handy compilations of facts, current statistics, names and addresses, and answers to the most frequently asked questions. These range from the venerable *Farmers Almanac, World Almanac,* and *Information Please Almanac* to specialized almanacs developed for special fields and industries. A good index is very critical in assessing these, since each almanac appears to pride itself in organizing its information differently and the table of contents is of limited value in locating specific information. Every small library needs at least one of these, and the library manager should examine the various common titles to determine which is most suitable. It is not essential for a small library to purchase a large number of almanacs. Special almanacs exist for many fields which cite chronologies, biographies, common addresses and telephone numbers, and these would be very essential for a library serving a specialized clientele. Almanacs should be replaced annually to ensure their contents are current.

Dictionaries

Probably the most fundamental reference book for every small library is a good unabridged dictionary. It will be the most heavily used reference book in the collection. There are numerous abridged and special dictionaries on the market, and the Reference Book section in *Booklist* reviews major new revisions as to their merit. Durable bindings are essential for every frequently consulted reference tool, and this is especially important in selecting an unabridged dictionary. Look for one that comes in a library binding, for it is worth the extra money. *Books in Print* will identify which titles come in that form. Some foreign language dictionaries may also be appropriate for the basic collection, as well as a good thesaurus. Dictionaries are not revised as frequently as many other types of reference books, but care should be taken to add or periodically replace them to ensure new terms are included.

Directories

These are among the most common reference tools. They include telephone books, industry and professional listings, and biographic resources like *Who's Who in America*. The most frequent questions received by most public libraries can be answered from their directory collection. A selection of telephone directories of nearby cities will prove popular, and if the parent organization has frequent contact with firms or individuals in specific cities located in other states, copies of these telephone directories should be purchased. The local telephone company can provide purchase information. Directories of all types do need to be regularly replaced to keep current with deaths, new additions, and address changes. Statisticians estimate that twenty percent of the residents of a typical city change addresses every year. Specialized directories should have multiple indexes to facilitate ease of access.

Indexes and Abstracts

An index is essential for the effective use of periodical collections and other special literature. The best examples are the *Readers Guide to Periodical Literature*, and the *Monthly Catalog of U.S. Government Publications.* However, there are a great number of more specialized indexes which cover the literature of certain fields, including *Library Literature.* A standard for selection should be the number of titles the library receives which are included in the index. A good index should contain standard and complete bibliographic entries and provide access by author, title and subject. Abstracts include brief summaries of the articles, in addition to the bibliographic citations, and these may be extremely valuable alternatives for those libraries that need to have access to the literature of selected field, but do not wish to maintain large subscription lists. However, abstracting tools as well as indexes may generate requests for books and periodical articles not in the library's collection.

Computerized Databases

Because many reference tools are developed in electronic form, more publishers are offering online and compact disk (CD-ROM) versions of their indexes, abstracts and other reference tools in addition to the print edition. The increased number of libraries using computers means that there is a growing market for these electronic products. Online computer databases offer libraries the advantage of rapid access to a current information, a variety of search options, and it may not be necessary to buy the print product. However, access to online databases require both a microcomputer and a modem, and training in how to search the database. Moreover, most online databases are not free. There is a charge for computer connect time and telecommunications. Despite these factors, there are hundreds of currently available online databases and the number is increasing rapidly. Many of these databases are bibliographic in content, but there are a growing number of databases which feature full text. Examples are *Books in Print Online, Mental Health Abstracts*, and the *U.S. Census.*

Several companies have been created to sell these online services, such as The Library Corporation, OCLC, and Information Access, to name only a few. These advertise in library publications and often exhibit at library conferences, and the library manager can contact them directly to determine which databases they offer, and their rates. They offer training, and a selection of enhancements that make searching and billing easier. Libraries should consider using online databases as an alternative or supplement to printed indexes when there is a need for current information and greater search capability.

Advice from The Frugal Librarian

The Frugal Librarian suggests that a good way to build a basic reference collection at low cost is to take advantage of book sales at library conferences. Many publishers exhibit at these events, and offer their display copies at discounts of twenty to fifty percent rather than ship the books back to their warehouse. A purchase order and (if the books are heavy) shipping may be required, but the savings will more than offset the trouble.

An alternative to online databases are CD-ROM (compact disk-read only memory) databases, which offer the convenience of computerized searching on the library's microcomputer while avoiding online costs. In place of the modem, however, the library must have a CD-ROM drive. Drives come in various speeds, and can accommodate multiple disks to avoid the necessity to make frequent changes. The speed and capacity required will depend on the number of CD-ROM databases owned by the library and on the frequency of use. However, CD-ROM databases have some drawbacks. They are only as current as the subscription updates, and there is still the necessity to gain familiarity with the search techniques and terms. Despite these limitations, CD-ROM databases are growing very popular with library users. There are hundreds of databases in CD-ROM format, ranging from encyclopedias to art libraries, and the prices are very competitive.

Reference Networks

OCLC and many state and regional networks offer specialized online databases for reference use as a service to their members, and the library manager should seek information on these options. These are primarily bibliographical databases, but other types of databases are constantly being added. Cooperative library systems often offer reference backup which may include online or CD-ROM database searches, and this may be an economical alternative for a small library. Libraries of a similar nature, such as medical libraries, often pool resources to develop online information networks and may have agreements regarding cooperative search and research services, as do their associations.

What Do You Do When You Do Not Have the Answer?

It is important to recognize that every library has its limitations, and cannot answer every question. The following alternatives should be considered when a reference question can't be answered using the library's own resources.

1. **Join a cooperative library system.** A common service to members is backup reference service for tough questions. Many of these systems are multitype, which means that any type and size of library may participate. There usually are some requirements, such as a willingness to loan materials from the collection. There may be some charges, but they are usually small, since many cooperative library systems are subsidized with state funds. Your state library agency can tell you whether there is a cooperative library system in your area.

2. **Contract with a larger library for backup reference service.** Many public and college libraries, and some special libraries are able and willing to enter into a contract that would let you refer reference questions to them. This may be an economical alternative since it permits use of their collection and professional librarians.

3. **If your parent organization is a member of a state or national professional or industrial association, check to determine what they have to offer.** Many associations offer research or library services, or maintain special computer databases as a benefit to their members, and may offer backup reference service. Many of the special library associations will also offer research service under certain conditions.

4) **Use information brokers.** These are free lance librarians or research firms that may either charge by the hour or on a per search basis for more specialized research. Many are skilled at online database searching, and they have access to other large library collections. The state library agency, cooperative library system, or large library usually has a list of these individuals or firms for referral purposes, and can share this information with you.

Resources

Balay, Robert, ed. *Guide to Reference Books*, 11th ed. Chicago: ALA, 1996. 2,000p.

Beckman, Robert. *Find It Fast: How To Uncover Expert Information on Any Subject.* 3rd rev. ed. New York: HarperCollins, 1994. 384p.

Bosch, Stephen, et al. *Guide to Selecting and Acquiring CD-ROMs, Software, and Other Electronic Publications.* Chicago: ALA, 1994. 64p.

Bruwelheide, Janis H. *The Copyright Primer for Librarians and Educators*, 2nd ed. Chicago: ALA, 1995. 160p.

Cassell, Kay Ann. *Developing Reference Collections and Services in an Electronic Age: A How-To-Do-It Manual for Librarians.* New York: Neal-Schuman, 1999. 150 p.

Childers, Thomas. *Information & Referral: Public Libraries.* Norwood, NJ: Ablex Publishing, 1984. 384p.

Dewey, Patrick. *301 CD-ROMs to Use in Your Library: Descriptions, Evaluations, and Practical Advice.* Chicago: ALA, 1996. 385p.

Katz, Bill, and Ruth A. Fraley, eds. *Evaluation of Reference Services.* Binghamton, NY: Haworth Press, 1985. 334p.

Katz, William A. *Introduction to Reference Work, Vol. I: Basic Information Services*, 6th ed. New York: McGraw, 1991.

Katz, Bill, ed. & comp. *Reference & Information Services: A Reader for the Nineties.* Metuchen, NJ: Scarecrow, 1991. 423p.

Kennedy, Scott, ed. *Reference Sources for Small & Medium-sized Libraries*, 6th ed. Chicago: ALA, 1999. 376p.

Kister, Kenneth. *Kister's Best Encyclopedias: A Guide to General & Specialized Encyclopedias*, 2nd ed. Phoenix, AZ: Oryx Press, 1994. 520p.

Martin, Murray S., and Betsy Park. *Charging and Collecting Fines and Fees: A Handbook for Libraries.* New York: Neal-Schuman, 1998. 146p.

Nichols, Margaret L. *Guide to Reference Books for School Library Media Centers.* Englewood, CO: Libraries Unlimited, 1992. 463p.

Patrick, Gay. *Building the Reference Collection: A How-to-Do-It Manual for School & Public Librarians.* New York: Neal-Schuman, 1992. 150p.

Pierce, Sydney J., ed. *Weeding & Maintenance of Reference Collections.* Binghamton, NY: Haworth Press, 1990. 183p.

Sader, Marion, and Amy Lewis, eds. *Encyclopedias, Atlases & Dictionaries.* New York: R.R. Bowker, 1995. 575p.

Safford, Barbara Ripp. *Guide to Reference Materials for School Library Media Centers*, 5th ed. Englewood, CO: Libraries Unlimited, 1998. 353p.

Walford, A., et al, eds. *Walford Guide to Reference Material.* 6th ed. London: Library Association Publishing, 1990-93, 2 vols.

Walker, Geraldene, and Joseph Janes. *Online Retrieval*, 2nd. Englewood, CO: Libraries Unlimited, 1999. 312p.

Wynar, Bohdan, eds. *Recommended Reference Books for Small & Medium-Sized Libraries and Media Centers.* Englewood, CO: Libraries Unlimited, 1999. 305p.

Recommended Reference Websites

Information Please Almanac
www.infoplease.com/

Old Farmers Almanac
www.almanac.com

CIA World Factbook
www.odci.gov/cia/
publications/factbook/
index.html

Mapquest
www.mapquest.com

Amazon.com
www.amazon.com

Historic Events and Birth Dates
www.scopesys. com/today/

OneLook Dictionaries
www.onelook.com/

Funk & Wagnalls Multimedia Encyclopedia
www.funkandwagnalls.com/

Learn2.com
www.learn2.com/index.html

Library of Congress
www.loc.gov

AnyWho
www.anywho.com/tf.html

Internet Public Library: Ready Reference Collection
www.ipl.org/ref/RR/

Interactive Weather Information Network
iwin.nws.noaa.gov/iwin/
graphicsversion/bigmain.html

Statistical Resources on the Web www.lib.umich.edu/
libhome/

U.S. Census Bureau Home Page www.census.gov/

United States Government Manual 1998/1999
www.access.gpo.gov/nara/
browse-gm.html

US Gazetteer
tiger.census.gov/cgi-bin/
gazetteer

US Postal Service Zip Codes
www.usps.gov/ncsc

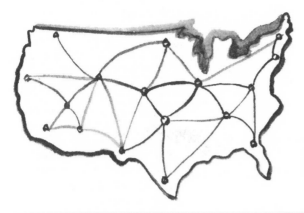

Borrowing Resources from Other Libraries

Chapter 8

Regardless of their library's size, managers soon realize the impracticality of seeking to purchase every recommended book and other library materials, even if cost and space were not constraining factors. Some books are of limited or special interest, and may be inappropriate for addition to the library's permanent collection. Some titles simply cannot be purchased because of limited distribution or other factors. Therefore, libraries are dependent upon one another to satisfy user requests for materials they will not be adding to their collections. Fortunately, there is a well-established process for accomplishing this, and that procedure is called interlibrary loan, or simply ILL.

Interlibrary loan is one of the most useful services a library can offer its users, and the library manager should promote greater awareness of this service among users. It is not a intended to be a substitute for an adequate collection, and libraries receiving frequent requests for specific titles should purchase them. However, it should be offered whenever the material the user is seeking cannot be found in the library's collection, and there is little or no likelihood the material will be purchased. During the past several decades, great advances have been made to simplify, standardize and improve access to other library collections. It should also be realized that there are some obligations the borrowing library assumes when it requests materials through interlibrary loan.

Interlibrary Loan Networks

Each state and major regions of the U.S. and many other nations have an interlibrary loan network, and these interface with other regional, national, and international interlibrary loan networks. They are often hierarchical, which means that if a book is not in the local library, the request should go to the state or regional ILL network, before it goes to the national network. The state library agency will advise the library manager regarding eligibility requirements for participation in this network, and how and where ILL requests should be sent. Many state and regional networks have automated the process so that requests will be automatically routed to those libraries that are most likely to have specified resources.

In the U.S. the effectiveness of the state, regional and national ILL networks is the result of a special partnership between the Library of Congress (LC) and the Online Library Computer Center (OCLC). Similar partnerships exist in other nations. In the U.S., when new books or other materials are published or produced, copies are sent to the Copyright Office at the LC. Depository copyright offices in other nations have a similar relationship with the national library. These materials are cataloged, and the records are added to a computerized catalog maintained by the national library and shared under special agreement with other organizations, such as OCLC. This information is provided online to thousands of member libraries throughout the world, who are able to use this bibliographic information to catalog copies of the titles they purchase. In the process of performing this function, the library adds its "holding" code.

It is therefore possible for a library to search this database and determine which libraries, at any point in time, own copies of a specific book or other resource. This information is provided to states and regional organizations, which are able to see that interlibrary loan requests are satisfied first within a given state or region, before the request is forwarded to another state, region, or even another nation.

Union Catalogs

Many states and regions have developed catalogs of the holdings of libraries within their geographic area, called union catalogs. Periodical holdings information is also collected in union lists of serial publications. Even libraries that do not use OCLC services can have their bibliographic records added to these union catalogs, and it is often a requirement that if a library participates in ILL at the state or regional level, that they will agree to contribute records to the union catalog, and make their resources available for loan to other libraries. State library agencies also seek to keep aware of subject specializations among the libraries in the state, so that even when a library has not added all of its holdings into the union catalog, ILL requests can be directed to a specific institution.

State and federal grant programs have often been used to strengthen the ILL process. For example, in the U.S., federal grants were awarded to large public libraries to strengthen their collections, provided that the materials purchased with these grants were cataloged, added to the state's union catalog, and made accessible through the ILL network to other libraries.

ILL Code

Because of the need for consistent procedures and the value associated with materials in the interlibrary loan procedure, a National Interlibrary Loan Code or policy has been developed in the U.S. by the American Library Association. Essentially it defines what materials may be requested through interlibrary loan, and describes the responsibilities of the borrowing and the lending libraries. Similar model ILL codes have been developed at the regional, state and local levels, and in other nations. The state library agency or cooperative library system serving your area can supply the applicable code. Libraries participating in ILL will generally be asked to adhere to this code.

Borrowing library's responsibilities usually include:

1 request only those materials which they are unlikely to purchase for their own collection,

2 adhere to standard ILL practices contained in the *Interlibrary Loan Practices Manual,*

3 inform users of their responsibilities to care for the materials borrowed,

4 comply with copyright regulations,

5 provide complete bibliographic information on the item in the request, and verify it using a standard reference tool,

6 screen and reject all ILL requests that do not comply with the Code,

7 use standard ILL formats in making the request *(see appendix D),*

8 use proper care in packing materials to be returned to the lending library, and pay for any delivery or mail costs and for any damage to the material, including replacement if the material is lost or cannot be repaired,

9 adhere to any special requirements the lending library may impose, and

10 encourage users to travel to other libraries whenever extensive use is required.

Loan periods are established by the lending library, which also retains the right to recall material at any time. Borrowing libraries also need to be aware that if they violate any provision of the Code, their future borrowing privileges are subject to suspension. While there is no national or international monitoring system, there is most certainly an informal network among libraries that will circulate information on institutions that do not comply with the Code.

Delivery

Many cooperative library systems, regional networks and state library agencies have delivery systems designed to link with the interlibrary loan network. This permits books and other materials to be delivered and returned as rapidly as possible. Sometimes these delivery systems use commercial delivery services as an alternative to their own delivery trucks. Telefacsimile is also used more frequently today for shorter documents such as journal articles because of the availability and convenience of this equipment. However, care must be taken to ensure that copyright violations do not occur in reproducing materials for transmission. When in doubt, contact the Copyright Clearance Center (222 Rosewood Dr., Danvers, MA 01923. Tel: 978/750-8400; E-mail: info@copyright.com; Web: www.copyright.com) or the publisher.

Costs

Borrowing libraries using ILL may experience some charges from the lending library. They are obligated to pay for any mailing expenses to and from the lending library, and the lending library may assess a reasonable handling charge. These charges tend to vary from one library to another. Some libraries are reimbursed by the state for their expenses, and others may absorb the costs in hope that other libraries will reciprocate when they request materials via ILL. Some libraries also ask the library user to pay these costs.

Standard ILL Form

The Code requires the use of a standard ILL form, which is available from all good library supply firms. This form requires the full bibliographic citation, which should always be verified in another standard bibliographic reference tool before the request is submitted. See appendix D for a sample ILL form.

Partnerships with Other Libraries

ILL only works when there is a willingness to cooperate fully with other libraries. Small libraries must be willing to lend to participate in interlibrary loan, and often they proportionately outlend larger libraries. Some states compensate libraries whenever there is an imbalance, but even when this does not occur, small libraries should be generous in honoring requests from other libraries. They are not required to loan materials which are proprietary in nature, rare, fragile or in heavy demand by their users.

It is also important to realize that to participate in ILL networks, libraries must be prepared to add their holdings to statewide and regional union catalogs in standard bibliographic form. Many states have programs and offer grants to facilitate this. Since this is usually required to be in machine read-

Lending library's responsibilities usually include:
1 to use its discretion in determining whether to comply with a request, but to be generous whenever possible,
2 to provide a statement of any special conditions, policies or charges to the borrowing library,
3 to promptly process ILL requests, and
4 to notify the borrowing library of any failures in compliance with the Code.

Materials which should not be requested via ILL are:
- rare or valuable material,
- bulky or fragile items that may be costly to ship or subject to damage,
- material likely to be in high demand, such as bestsellers,
- materials which are unlikely to be loaned at the local level, such as reference books or proprietary materials, and
- unique materials that would be difficult or impossible to replace if they were lost in delivery.

able form, this represents another reason why small libraries should give careful consideration to using a computer in their operations. Computerization makes it relatively easy to submit current holdings information, and eventually to add older records through what is known as a retrospective conversion.

Partnerships with Other Community Organizations

Although the focus of this chapter is upon interlibrary cooperation, consideration should also be given to establishing cooperative programs and agreements with other nonprofit and private institutions and organizations. Shared use of space, personnel, equipment, technical and other expertise can save valuable time and funds, especially for small libraries. An initial investment of time may be required to develop standard policies and procedures, and some compromises are usually required, but the results will include better service to the library's users.

Following are some of the basic principles to consider in developing collaborative partnerships with other organizations: (1) Develop partnerships that contribute to your library's mission and goals. Remember that your time and resources are limited, and that you need to continuously evaluate whether joint projects will yield long-range benefits. (2) Make certain that your supervisor or governance understands and supports your participation in the partnership. (3) Develop formal agreements for long-term cooperative programs. Many collaborative activities are developed informally by "handshake." That might be acceptable in the short term, but it could lead to misunderstandings in the long term. To avoid problems, especially when funds and personnel are involved, consider preparing a written agreement that clearly states the individual and mutual obligations and policies. (4) Involve staff in developing cooperative policies and procedures. Many problems can be avoided if the people who have to implement a cooperative activity have an active role in planning how the program will work. (5) In developing any cooperative program, remain flexible, and be willing to compromise.

Library managers who are interested in developing cooperative programs will find practical guidance in *The Librarian's Guide to Partnerships,* edited by Sherry Lynch (Highsmith Press, 1999). The contributors objectively describe the pros and cons of different types of collaborative programs, how they developed the projects, and what results were achieved.

Advice from The Frugal Librarian

While interlibrary loan can be a wonderful service to offer library users, some individuals may abuse it by requesting numerous titles because they anticipate few titles will be loaned by other libraries. The Frugal Librarian suggests that patrons be asked to complete an ILL form for each book requested, and that they be notified of the average costs and success rate for ILL requests for selected categories of materials. While the bibliographic information will still need to be verified and completed by the staff, it will save some time. The cost and fulfillment information, and involvement in the process may also lead the patron to be more selective in terms of his requests.

Resources

Bajjaly, Stephen. *The Librarian's Community Network Handbook.* Chicago: ALA, 1999. 216p.

Boucher, Virginia. *Interlibrary Loan Practices Handbook* 2nd ed. Chicago: ALA, 1995. 250p.

Harloe, Bart, ed. *Guide to Cooperative Collection Development.* Chicago: ALA, 1994. 48p.

Kachel, Debra E. *Collection Assessment and Management for School Libraries: Preparing for Cooperative Collection Development.* Westport, CT: Greenwood, 1997. 224p.

Lynch, Sherry, ed. *The Librarian's Guide to Partnerships.* Ft. Atkinson, WI: Highsmith Press, 1999. 100p. A complete guide to cooperative agreements with schools, corporations, colleges, and other public services.

Morris, Leslie R. *Interlibrary Loan Policies Directory,* 6th ed. New York: Neal-Schuman, 1999. 1,286p.

Serving Your Users

Chapter 9

Knowing who the library's users are, what they need, and how to better serve them are among the primary responsibilities of every library manager. Because many libraries are likely to have more than one type of user, and many users are likely to have differing needs, this is not a simple task. For example, school and college libraries have students and faculty, public libraries have children and adults, and so forth. Collections and services need to be designed to meet the diverse requirements of these individuals, and staff need to be sensitive to the fact that the library's users and their needs will certainly change in the future.

Children and Young Adults

Children and young adult users need resources that have appropriate reading levels and are on topics that are of particular interest to their age group. While it is generally advisable to avoid separate divisions of the collection and user areas in a small library, it is usual for libraries serving youth and adults to divide the collection accordingly. Shelving in areas devoted to youth is usually 48"–60" high, and chairs and tables need to be of a size suitable for youth. Some other special equipment may be required, such as picture book shelving. Some libraries integrate adult and children's nonfiction, because it will allow a richer collection to be available to both adults and children. When this is done, and adult height shelving is used, care must be taken to have movable stools so youth can reach upper shelves.

Programming for youth is also an important responsibility. Story hours introduce children to reading. A specialist who can work with children and young adults, select resources for them, and undertake appropriate programming is highly recommended. This is often one of the first positions that are added to libraries when the budget permits.

Young adult collections are usually a mix of adult and children's titles, although there are many fiction and nonfiction works written expressly for this age level. It is an extremely important time for youth, as they make the transition between childhood and adult responsibilities. Materials need to be

> The goal of children's library services is to introduce reading and learning to each child, and to set the foundation for their appreciation and enjoyment of books and media in the future.

carefully selected that help to develop their reading skills and provide them with useful guidance in dealing with peer pressures, family relationships, sexuality and career planning. Many larger public libraries and school systems have specialists in young adult literature and services, and these should be contacted if your library has a young adult clientele. They can suggest selection tools and other resources appropriate for this age level.

Adult Services

Regrettably, some libraries assume that adults do not require special services or programs, and that they can fend for themselves. That is unfortunate, for some adults may have come from another country or a region where libraries are uncommon. Some adults have disabilities which require alternative library material such as large print or talking books. Adults who are unfamiliar with the literature of a special field may need guidance in their research or study. In summary, every library serving adults has an obligation to plan and implement services and programs designed to meet the specialized needs of this clientele.

A starting point for identifying these needs and planning appropriate adult services is the library's advisory committee. An informal survey of the library's adult users is another method. Essentially, the manager needs to identify the types of users, their level of familiarity with library resources, and what sort of service and resources they will require. The manager should neither underestimate nor overestimate adult user needs. Many may be unfamiliar with good library service and have a low level of expectation. Others may have used large research libraries, and have unreasonably high expectations.

Generally, adult library services consist of orientation, readers' advisory assistance, specialized individual services and group services. Schools and colleges traditionally offer library orientations and training programs in library research, and it may be appropriate for special and public libraries to consider similar activities based on the nature of the library's use and the needs of its adult clientele. Libraries are educational institutions, and the library manager should always bear this in mind. Adults entering into a new field of study or work may also require guidance in the specialized literature of that field. A good example might be a firm starting a new research and development program. Consideration might be given to contracting with a scholar or research librarian to provide a training program or consultant assistance in developing this portion of the collection.

Many libraries identify the specialized needs of individual users by referral or survey. For example, the staff of a church or synagogue library may learn of a homebound elderly adult, who may have a visual handicap. This may necessitate a visit to identify reading interests, the identification of a volunteer to deliver and pick-up materials, and the purchase of large print books. Group services are often programmatic in nature, such as the design of a travel film series for a nursing home, or the development of a literacy program for a jail, in cooperation with a group such as the Literacy Volunteers of America. Design of these group services may require some specialized expertise, and the library manager should consider cooperation with another institution that may have needed experience. Exhibits and displays

A major goal in serving young adults is to maintain and increase their awareness of library resources and appreciation of reading and learning. Many young adults stop using libraries when they leave school, and they lose a valuable resource for their future growth.

Advice from The Frugal Librarian

Book displays and exhibits, and library programs for children and adults are important activities, but unfortunately, good exhibits and programs can take time that a small library may not have. The Frugal Librarian suggests that libraries pool their displays and programs and share them. Many exhibits can be designed for travel, and program presenters may be willing to travel a reasonable distance to repeat a successful program.

of new books is another form of programming many small libraries may use to inform or educate their adult users regarding new resources, although this is often considered library promotion.

Services to Persons with Disabilities

Services to person with disabilities is of great importance, and libraries have a legal and moral obligation in this area of service. In the U.S. the Americans with Disabilities Act (ADA) requires that libraries of all types design services, programs and collections appropriate for individuals who may have special needs. The manager must see that there are no physical barriers that affect access to collections and services. Special equipment may be required, and information in special formats might be needed.

It is very important to design the library and collection so that the facilities are welcoming and the staff understands how to effectively serve disabled patrons. If the library does not have a ground level entrance, a ramp may be required to eliminate this barrier. If the library's collection and services are located on more than one level, elevator access is needed. In some states, federal or state grants are available to improve access for the disabled, and the state library agency or cooperative library system can provide information on eligibility. Rest rooms must also be designed so they are accessible to individuals in wheelchairs. High shelving with narrow aisles is also a problem for persons in wheelchairs. Aisles should be wide enough to allow for wheelchair access, and extension clamping devices should be provided.

A critical factor in giving good service to physically challenged patrons is staff attitude. Most staff will realize that disabled persons are entitled to the same services and courtesy as all other library users. However, some staff may seek to overcompensate in serving disabled users. A number of excellent training materials have been developed to aid staff in understanding how to effectively serve users with disabilities, and these are cited at the end of this chapter. Consideration should be given to either purchasing or borrowing these via interlibrary loan, to aid staff in gaining confidence in serving these users. If the library has an advisory committee composed of users it would also be excellent if at least one of the users represented the disabled.

Good library suppliers will offer catalogs containing equipment, furnishings and other resources to better serve disabled persons. Tables that can accommodate wheelchairs, magnifiers for visually handicapped patrons, and a telephone with amplification for hearing impaired persons are examples of the type of resource that will be of great value. In many instances, where only limited funding exists for equipment or training, some simple alternatives can be employed. For example, if no staff member knows sign language for serving hearing impaired patrons, the simple expedient of keeping a pad of paper and pencil handy at each service desk would be valuable. Several resource books on how to serve persons with specific types of disabilities, ranging from developmental to physical, are listed at the end of this chapter.

Outreach

Extension of services may be appropriate for some small libraries in reaching certain types of users. A good example would be a hospital library which pro-

National Library Service

One of the major agencies to aid visually disabled library users in the U.S. is the National Library Service (NLS), located at the Library of Congress in Washington, DC.

NLS maintains a network of regional and subregional libraries located in each state. By contacting the state library agency, the address and telephone number of the nearest regional or subregional library can be obtained. Any individual who is permanently or even temporarily visually disabled can be referred to these agencies and become eligible for recorded books or braille materials, as well as necessary equipment to listen to the recordings. Materials for the visually handicapped can be sent through the U.S. Postal Service postage free.

Many periodicals are also available in recorded format. The regional or subregional library can inform the visually handicapped user whether there is a radio reading service in the area or other volunteer assistance programs. Radio reading services often read the contents of the daily newspapers and other materials which may not be available in audio or braille form.

vides a small collection of books on child care and development in the maternity or pediatric wards for use by parents. Every library needs to consider this in the context of the accessibility of its collection to its potential users, and existing barriers or space limitations.

However, it is generally recommended that managers avoid "branch" collections because of the difficulty of maintaining them, and the cost of duplicate materials or additional staff. Public libraries, for example, should not consider creating branch libraries until population exceeds 25,000 persons, unless major physical barriers or large geographic service areas exist. It is better to centralize collections and services, because it avoids unnecessary duplication in the collection, staffing and facilities. Special libraries serve smaller groups, and usually provide a more intensive level of service, but special library associations often have guidelines or standards, and these can be found by consulting the literature on library service in that specialized field, through contacts with similar types of library, or be contacting qualified consultants who might be available at the state library agency or the cooperative library system in the area.

Measurement and Evaluation

The library manager has a variety of options in measuring the effectiveness of service to users. These include maintenance of statistics, periodic user surveys, advisory committees, assessment of progress on long range plans, or simply by asking the users over the service desk. Often, a combination of several methods are used. Whatever methods are employed, care should be taken to ensure that the collection of statistics does not become time consuming. If the manager is taking over operation of an existing library, the existing statistical tabulation methods should be evaluated. A good rule is to collect only those statistics and evaluative information which will actually be used to improve services and collections. Sometimes, information is collected to satisfy a special need, and it may continue to be collected long after the need has past.

Generally, libraries should retain basic information on their collection, usage and users. This would include the size of the collection, including a breakdown by format (i.e., books, tapes, periodicals, etc.). Usage would include circulation of materials, reference questions received and answered, interlibrary loan requests, and number of users. Consideration should be given to taking samples of usage. For example, experience has shown that reference statistics tabulated during a typical week are reasonably accurate in projecting total usage for the year when they are multiplied by the number of weeks the library is open for service. An excellent resource on measurement and evaluation is *Output Measures for Public Libraries* which is cited at the end of this chapter.

Probably one of the easiest and most effective evaluation methods is to consider user purchase recommendations for books and other resources. Installing a suggestion box has helped many library managers to identify needed resources. If a less formal method is desirable, the library manager should ensure that users are aware that their recommendations are welcome.

Advice from The Frugal Librarian

A simple variation on the suggestion box is the "post-it" bulletin board. The Frugal Librarian suggests mounting a small cork board with a supply of thumb tacks, cards, and a pen anchored to the board. Post a note asking for suggestions (anonymous or signed), and "salt" the board with a few interesting suggestions. Be sure to regularly check the board, and be certain to promptly respond to each posted suggestion or concern. Many library managers find this a quick and easy way to gain input ranging from purchase suggestions to policy revisions.

Hint: Some libraries may be asked to keep selected statistics for the state library agency or for some other organization to be used in directories or for comparative purposes. Whenever this information is provided, a copy of this information should be retained, since it may be useful in responding to other inquiries or surveys.

Resources

Alire, Camila, and Orlando Archibeque. ***Serving Latino Communities.*** New York: Neal-Schuman, 1998. 255p.

Benson, Allen C., and Linda Fodemski. ***Connecting Kids and the Internet: A Handbook for Librarians, Teachers, and Parents.*** 2nd ed. New York: Neal-Schuman, 1999. 375p.

Davis, Robin Works. ***Toddle On Over: Developing Infant & Toddler Literature Programs.*** Ft. Atkinson, WI: Highsmith Press, 1998. 96p.

Deines-Jones, Courtney, and Connie Van Fleet. ***Preparing Staff to Serve Patrons With Disabilities.*** New York: Neal-Schuman, 1995. 160pp.

Foos, Donald and Nancy Pack. ***How Libraries Must Comply with the Americans with Disabilities Act (ADA).*** Phoenix, AZ: Oryx Press, 1992. 192p.

Greene, Ellin. ***Books, Babies and Libraries: Serving Infants, Toddlers, Their Parents & Caregivers.*** Chicago: ALA, 1991. 186p.

James, Helen Foster. ***Across the Generations: Building Understanding Through Intergenerational Literature.*** Ft. Atkinson, WI: Highsmith Press, 1996. 120p.

Jones, Patrick. ***Connecting Young Adults and Libraries: A How-to-Do-It Manual for Librarians.*** 2nd ed. New York: Neal-Schuman, 1998. 461p.

Karp, Rashelle. ***Library Services for Disabled Individuals.*** Boston: G.K. Hall, 1991. 119p.

Miller, Glenn. ***Customer Service & Innovation in Libraries.*** Ft. Atkinson, WI: Highsmith Press, 1996. 93p.

People First: Serving and Employing People with Disabilities. Towson, MD: Library Video Network, 1990. 38 min. 1/2" videotape.

Smith, Kitty. ***Serving the Difficult Customer.*** New York: Neal-Schuman, 1994. 166p.

Totten, Herman, and Risa Brown. ***Culturally Diverse Library Collections for Children.*** New York: Neal-Schuman, 1994. 299 p.

Trotta, Marcia. ***Managing Library Outreach Programs: A How-to-Do-It Manual for Librarians.*** New York: Neal-Schuman, 1993. 150 p.

Van House, Nancy, et al. ***Output Measures for Public Libraries: A Manual of Standardized Procedures,*** 2nd ed. Chicago: ALA, 1987. 99 p.

Walter, Virginia. ***Output Measures for Public Library Service to Children: A Manual of Standardized Procedures.*** Chicago: ALA, 1992. 129p.

Wright, Kieth, and Judith Davie. ***Serving the Disabled.*** New York: Neal- Schuman, 1991. 161p.

Filtering

One of the most difficult issues facing many libraries that serve youth is whether to limit access to the Internet. Because filtering software has been developed that claims to block access to pornographic sites, libraries in some communities have been asked to install it. Some state and federal officials have also demanded that libraries be required to install this software in order to receive state or federal funds.

This is creating both a philosophical and a practical quandary for libraries. Unfortunately, there is no universal solution to this problem. Some libraries have decided to allow open access, and some have limited access, based on community values and concerns. Other strategies include:

1) Installation of filters on selected computers. Children can use only filtered computers, unless their paents sign a release.

2) Installation of special search engines or bookmarked websites. Some search engines such as Yahooligans (www.yahooligans.com) have selected websites that meet criteria appropriate for youth.

3) Place computers with access to the Internet in prominent locations, with posted policies prohibiting access to adults-only sites. If the staff observe youth accessing pornographic sites, they will require adherence to the library's policies, or bar youth from further access.

Your Library's Human Resources

Chapter 10

The most important resource in any library is its staff. They are also likely to be the largest part of any library's budget, and for that reason we have stressed methods to make the most effective use of their time in this book. There are several basic tools that every library manager should have to ensure the fair and effective supervision of its staff: an organization chart, staff policy handbook, job descriptions and a compensation plan. These tools will also aid in avoiding legal difficulties if personnel problems should arise.

If the library is part of an organization that already has these tools, the library manager should check to ensure that the larger organization's policies take the library's unique working conditions into consideration, and see that amendments are made if the policies do not reflect the library's work requirements. For example, library hours may extend beyond the normal work day for the organization, requiring different work standards for library staff. It is also likely that the library's positions may have unique requirements compared to other positions in the organization.

A good staff policy handbook contains background on the organization and its mission, describes essential work rules such as staff hours and policies on absence or tardiness, and usually summarizes employee benefits. It may also include key names and telephone numbers for referral. If the library manager must develop such a document, it should be reviewed by the organization's personnel manager and legal counsel to ensure it is accurate and that it conforms to the organization's policies and practices. A sound personnel practice every manager should follow is to schedule an orientation for each new employee to review the manual, and to answer any questions or concerns. Every library employee should receive a copy, and it should be regularly reviewed to ensure it is current. Another library of similar size or type may be willing to loan a copy of their handbook to provide a starting point.

Job descriptions should be developed for every position in the library, including part-time and volunteer staff, if such positions exist. Job descriptions may take many forms, and the library manager should follow the form

> An **organizational chart** is a graphic means of showing the reporting relationships and responsibilities within an institution or firm.
>
> Library Manager
>
> Circulation   Reference
> Clerk   Assistant

used by their parent organization, provided one exists. The job title should be as standard as possible, since this will help in defining the appropriate salary level when the position is compared with other titles in the organization or in other libraries. Many state library associations have developed simple standard job descriptions which are suitable for a wide range of libraries, and these may provide a starting point.

In listing the typical duties, care should be taken to cite that these are illustrative, and that "other duties may be assigned" by the supervisor. The job requirements that are specified should be those which are reasonable for the position, and not be so specialized that they become discriminatory. Again, job descriptions should be reviewed by the parent organization's legal counsel and personnel officer to avoid conflicts with the organization's policies. It is also highly recommended that when a new job description is written for existing employees, that they be given an opportunity to review the document to verify accuracy and to gain their input. A part of the orientation procedure for all new employees should feature a review of the job description.

The development of an employee compensation plan is a complex task. If the parent organization does not have a plan, the manager would be wise to seek expert assistance. A compensation plan consists of a salary and/or wage schedule and fringe benefits. Because of state and federal requirements governing both wages and benefits, and the potential fiscal impact of benefits such as health insurance and retirement, care must be taken to ensure that the library's compensation plan is legal and financially sound, in addition to being fair and competitive in attracting qualified personnel. Managers of many small libraries often hire part-time or temporary personnel with the assumption that these positions are exempt from consideration under compensation plans, but legal rulings and federal and state regulations are steadily extending coverage.

Consultant help for the development of a compensation plan is available in almost every community. Most management consulting firms offer compensation planning assistance, and personnel officers from other libraries and organizations may also be willing to extend assistance on a contract or hourly basis. The library manager needs to ensure that the parent organization's governance or administration is involved in any decision making. Furthermore, the manager needs to ensure that the plan provides for compensation that is fair and sufficient to attract the quality of personnel essential for the library's mission. While cost must be considered in the development of any plan, the library's personnel deserve wages and benefits comparable to those received by other staff in the parent organization or in similar libraries who perform similar work.

The One-Person Library

When there is only one person operating a library, it is very easy to become overwhelmed with the responsibilities. Libraries are labor intensive, and there are everyday routines that can absorb enormous amounts of valuable time. The manager of the one-person library has to be well organized and exercise discipline in avoiding routines which may be very comfortable, but which steal time from the library's basic mission, which is to serve its users.

Job Descriptions

A good job description should contain the following basic elements:

- exact job title
- a brief description of the basic requirements or purpose of the job,
- a listing of typical duties, essential and desirable requirements,
- who the position reports to, and
- which positions are supervised by that position.

Advice from The Frugal Librarian

Many local, regional, state, and provincial library associations undertake salary surveys for their member libraries. The Frugal Librarian suggests that membership in an association that collects this information may be a wise and economical step, avoiding the cost of consultant assistance, and ensuring that staff are neither under nor overpaid. The trick is to ensure that comparable job titles and responsibilities are used in the survey and in your library.

While the manager may not be able to delegate routine work to other staff, there may be some indirect delegation that can occur, such as buying books and other materials already cataloged and processed. If the library is part of a parent organization, other departments may be able to assume some portion of the library's routines. For example, the mail room may be able to process and shelve periodicals, or route them to individuals in the organization. An administrative pool may be able to handle orders or maintain certain files or indexes. Approval will obviously be needed from the supervisors of those departments, but they may be willing to assume these routine duties which would allow better work flow, and which would gain valuable time for the library manager.

Don't forget the microcomputer!

There are a growing number of software products designed for libraries, and they can save many hours of work, effectively maintain important records, and substantially improve library service. A good example is periodical routing, which is service offered by many small libraries to special users. Checking in new periodicals, filing claims for missing numbers, and seeing that current titles are routed to users in an organization could become a time-killer, depending on the number of magazines and the routing complexity. However, relatively inexpensive microcomputer software has been developed by many firms to permit check-in to be quickly accomplished, including the generation of routing slips and the generation of claim forms for missing numbers. These software packages are regularly displayed at library conferences, and they are advertised in library publications, as well as being sold by reputable library suppliers.

However, the best advice the manager of a one-person library can follow is not to assume any routine that does not contribute to the library's mission and effective user service. As a small unit in a larger organization, the library may "inherit" miscellaneous duties delegated by higher management. Usually this occurs because the role and mission of the library may not be understood by others in the organization. These delegated responsibilities may have nothing to do with the library, and the library manager may be inclined to accept them in order to accommodate higher management, or simply because the additional duty does not appear to require significant time.

Adding or Replacing Staff

Eventually even the smallest library will be faced with the need to add or replace personnel. If the library is not part of a parent organization with its own personnel department and procedures, the library manager will need to follow several basic guidelines in recruiting, interviewing and selecting personnel. The first is to ensure that a job description exists that is current and accurate, and to use it for preparation of recruiting materials. The library's compensation plan should also define the wage and benefits for the position. It is never sound practice to advertise or recruit for a position unless either a salary range or a specific wage and benefits are established. It may be the practice of the library or its parent organization not to cite the wage in the advertisement, or to list it as "open" or "negotiable," but if that is the case, the specific wage or range should be stated in the interview with each applicant.

Advice from The Frugal Librarian

It may be very difficult to reject an assigned new responsibility, even when it is clearly inappropriate. If that should occur, the Frugal Librarian suggests that the best strategy a manager can take is to review the library's responsibilities, work load, and the manager's job description with upper management to see how this new assignment can be handled. Upper management should view this as a conscientious effort to ensure that the responsibility is effectively planned, and they may conclude that the work would be more appropriate in another unit after they understand more about the library.

Recruitment for any position in the library should be as open as possible to ensure the best possible applicant pool. If it is the practice of the parent organization to offer positions first to internal candidates, the notice should be posted with a description of the job and the library manager's name and telephone number cited as a source for additional information. If the library uses volunteers, they should also be invited to consider application. If applicants outside of the organization are to be considered, advertisements in local newspapers should be placed, particularly in publications that reach minority communities. Today, every organization has an obligation, both legally and morally, to develop a culturally diverse workforce, to ensure that persons with disabilities are given opportunities, and to avoid any discrimination based on age, gender, race, religious or ethnic background, or sexual preference.

Another basic form the library requires is an employment application, assuming that the parent organization does not have one. This is an essential document which will help provide basic information in evaluating the qualifications of the applicants, and will save considerable time in the interview. While some organizations rely on resumes or written letters of application, the applicant may omit key information, and design the letter or resume to hide gaps in employment. Employment forms may be borrowed from other organizations in the community that have a reputation for sound personnel practices as a basis for comparison. Because certain questions may not be asked either on an employment form or during the interview, such as age, the library manager should confer with the organization's attorney or personnel officer, and have them review the form before it is used. A good employment form collects vital information such as address, experience and training. The individual should also be asked to formally sign the form, to verify that the information he/she supplied on the application is correct.

Interviewing candidates should always be done privately, and if the library manager does not have a separate office, a conference room or another office should be borrowed for the occasion. Care should be taken to ensure that every candidate is warmly welcomed, and following a brief overview of the job, the applicant should be given an opportunity to ask questions about the position. The interviewer might follow this discussion by reviewing the application form with the candidate to resolve any questions, such as missing information. The interviewer should use open ended questions whenever possible, to gain additional information needed to evaluate both strengths and weaknesses.

As a basic courtesy, all candidates should be notified of the outcome. It is sufficient to thank the candidates for their interest in the position, and to notify them that another applicant was selected. It is also be advisable to inform the candidates that their applications will be retained on file for a specified period in the event another vacancy should occur, unless it is not the policy of the parent organization to do this. Applicants who are selected for a position should be formally notified in writing, and the notice should clearly state the compensation, starting date and supervisor. Some organizations also require a written acceptance from the candidate. It is customary to note any conditions, and a probation period is usually one of the conditions.

Always Include These Three Interview Questions

1. Candidates should be asked why they are interested in the position, for this will allow them to summarize personal goals and correlate them to the position.

2. Candidates should be asked to explain how their experience, training and interests qualifies for the work, for the question will allow each individual to discuss their strengths.

3. The interviewer needs to determine the availability of the candidate, and whether the compensation would be satisfactory.

Some candidates may not know when to stop talking, and in those situations the Frugal Librarian strongly recommends that the interviewer be more directive. Make certain the candidate knows that you have gained sufficient information regarding their qualifications. Thank him/her for their time and interest in the job, and indicate that you must move on to another obligation.

This may range between 30 to 360 days, and it should be understood that if performance is not satisfactory, employment will terminated.

Evaluating Performance

The performance of every library employee should be regularly evaluated. This is customarily more frequently done during the probationary period of new employees, and done on an annual basis for all other employees.

Once again, if the library has a parent organization, it may have specific policies and forms for evaluation. If not, a special form does not need to be developed. The library manager can use the employee's job description as a basis for performance evaluation. This document defines the primary responsibilities and typical duties of each job, and the manager can prepare a brief assessment in writing, defining where strengths exist, and where improvements are needed. A time for a private discussion should be determined, and the employee should be provided a copy of the performance evaluation in advance of the meeting to allow time for study.

The manager should be prepared to review the evaluation at this meeting, and determine if clarification is needed. The manager should use this meeting to discuss any new goals or assignments, and identify how the supervisor can be of further assistance to the employee, such as providing further training.

Resolving Personnel Problems

Good selection and evaluation procedures will go far to avoid or reduce personnel problems, but it is inevitable that every organization will experience some problems. The manager of a small library needs to become aware of friction and other performance problems, and discuss them privately with the pertinent staff member as soon as they are observed. Never criticize or discipline employees in front of their co-workers or library users.

If a serious problem occurs, every staff member deserves the time and opportunity to correct the deficiency. They deserve an clear definition of the problem and your assistance in avoiding it in the future. This is known as due process. It is usually difficult to criticize performance and interpersonal conflicts, and some supervisors ignore these problems in hope they will disappear. They may not, and the effective library manager has an obligation to deal with these problems before they affect the library and its services to users. If the staff member does not correct the deficiencies following reasonable notice, the manager should consider other disciplinary steps the parent organization has defined, and if those fail, proceed with termination, rather than accept substandard performance.

Volunteers

Many small nonprofit libraries benefit through the contributions of volunteers, and every library manager should consider recruiting and developing these valuable human resources. Many organizations are able to develop programs and services which could not normally be considered without the special talents and skills of volunteers, and the volunteers also benefit because of the enrichment they bring to others. Some volunteers can gain valuable experience that may qualify them for regular employment. Many schools and

---

Cardinal Rules for Personnel Management in the Small Library

There are many factors to success in operating a small library, but the most important involve personnel. The following suggestions are offered.

Hire the best staff possible.
Take care in selecting people who enjoy service to others, and who genuinely are interested in what the library can do.

Invest in training the library staff and yourself.
It will strengthen the organization's most important resource, and it is a great morale builder for the staff.

Deal with problems fairly and promptly.
Ignoring personnel problems is a disservice to staff and the library's users.

Do not allow routine to rule the library.
Keep the staff aware of the library's mission and responsibilities to users.

There are many ways to motivate personnel, but the best ways are fair and competitive compensation, and personal recognition and appreciation for good performance.

service organizations require their students or members to participate in community service projects, and the small library can take advantage of this opportunity. Volunteers can also be the library's best public relations device, for they will know of the library's potential, and they will tell others about it.

Some managers are reluctant to use volunteers because they believe it is too difficult to train them, and they anticipate volunteers are unreliable. The truth of the matter is that volunteers are no more difficult to train than regular staff members. Some volunteers may be unreliable, but there are techniques for effective volunteer management that will weed them out. First of all, it should be realized that volunteers need most of the same things that are provided to staff. They need to be trained and have well defined responsibilities. They need guidance and evaluation, and most especially, they need some recognition and a sense of accomplishment.

Libraries with a significant number of volunteers should designate one of them as coordinator, preferably the individual with the best organizational skills. A regular schedule should be established for each volunteer, and the library manager should develop a recognition program in cooperation with this coordinator and the parent organization's governance or administration. While there are many different ways to recognize volunteer contributions, the best methods are personal appreciation, and the development of assignments that are challenging and rewarding to the individual volunteers.

Resources

Bailey, Martha J. *The Special Librarian As a Supervisor or Middle Manager*, 2nd ed. Washington, DC: Special Libraries Association, 1986. 176p.

Black, William K., ed. *Libraries & Student Assistants: Critical Links*. Binghamton, NY: Haworth Press, 1995. 176p.

Caputo, Janette. *Stress and Burnout in Library Service*. Phoenix, AZ: Oryx Press, 1991. 184p.

Cochran, J. Wesley. *Time Management Handbook for Librarians*. Westport, CT: Greenwood, 1991. 160p.

Dragich, Martha J. and Peter C. Schanck, eds. *Law Library Staff Organization & Administration*. Littleton, CO: Rothman, 1990. 238p.

Farmer, Leslie. *Training Student Library Staff*. Worthington, OH: Linworth Press, 1997. 183p.

Giesecke, Joan. *Practical Help for New Supervisors*. 3rd ed. Chicago: ALA, 1997. 117p.

Martin, Lowell. *Library Personnel Administration*. Lanham, MD: Scarecrow Press, 1994. 214p.

Platz, Valerie Anna, and Charles Kratz, eds. *The Personnel Manual: An Outline for Libraries*. rev. ed. Chicago: ALA, 1993. 96p.

Rooks, Dana C. *Motivating Today's Library Staff: A Management Guide*. Phoenix, AZ: Oryx Press, 1988. 184p.

Rubin, Richard. *Hiring Library Employees*. New York: Neal-Schuman, 1993. 209p.

St. Clair, Guy, and Joan Williamson. *Managing the New One-Person Library*, 2nd ed. New Providence, NJ: K. G. Saur, 1992.

Stueart, Robert, and Maureen Sullivan. *Performance Analysis and Appraisal*. New York: Neal-Schuman, 1991. 174p.

Switzer, Teri R. *Safe At Work? Library Security and Safety Issues*. Lanham, MD: Scarecrow Press, 1999. 208p.

Webb, Gisela M., ed. *Human Resources Management in Libraries*. Binghamton, NY: Haworth Press, 1989. 130p.

Service Learning

One national trend that has implications for libraries involves youth volunteers. Some school systems and youth organizations are requiring students to contribute their time to community organizations such as libraries. This community experience is called Service Learning.

If your library could benefit from a teen volunteer program, the following suggestions might assist in making the program more effective for everyone involved:

Take the time to contact local school authorities to determine whether they have a service learning program. If so, schedule a meeting with the individual in charge to learn more about their goals and policies.

Make certain that sufficient time is provided to effectively train student volunteers for meaningful service. Some programs require only ten or twelve hours of community service, and school officials need to know this is insufficient to prepare students. Develop a written agreement that addresses the mutual and individual responsibilities of the school and the library. For example, what type of evaluations will the school require, and will their liability insurance extend to the library.

Involve the staff in planning a variety of interesting assignments for the teen volunteers. Involving them in this process will gain their commitment to the program. Have patience in training and supervising the teens. This may be their first work experience, and they may need very basic guidance, such as remembering who to call if they will be late for a volunteer assignment.

Be certain to recognize and thank each teen volunteer for their contribution. This will affect their future opinion about the library.

Developing Your Library

Chapter 11

A library that does not have a plan to continue its improvement and strengthen its collections and services to users in the future will eventually fail. New library resources are continually being developed. Funds will be needed to acquire them, and space will be needed to accommodate them. Users will change, and their information needs will evolve. Specialized furnishings or equipment are likely to be required. Additional staff may be needed as usage grows, or existing staff will require new skills to better or more effectively serve the library's clientele.

Start With a Vision

The process of developing a library begins the moment it is first organized, and it should continue for as long as the library exists. As the manager reviews the original plan created for the library, new goals and objectives should be identified for the future, based on the manager's assessment of the rate of growth in funding, usage, and the evolving mission of the library. Simply put, the manager needs to start with a vision of what the library will be five to ten years in the future, and regularly revise that vision as resources are found, and challenges arise.

The vision may be based on some other library the manager may have seen or used, or it may be based on the mission and original goals of its advisory committee or those who were responsible starting the library. Or it may come from some entirely different source, such as additional training the manager may have received.

Library development begins with a vision and a plan for implementation. Vision is derived from the manager's initial training, experience and values, and it is enriched and refreshed by contacts with users, sensitivity to need, reading, further training and interchange with advisory groups, supervisors and other library managers. The planning process was discussed in chapter 2, and the library manager must remember that the process is continuous, participatory, and an essential part of the manager's job.

However, there are two aspects of development which must receive the

There are many factors which contribute to the success of a library, but good libraries all have several things in common.

First, the management, staff and governance have a common vision of what the library will become in the future.

Second, they must have the commitment to reach that goal.

Third, and most important, there has to be leadership with the courage and ability to articulate that vision.

attention of every manager. Without adequate financial resources, no library can either operate effectively or improve its services and collections. Accordingly, this chapter will offer some strategies and suggestions on financial development. The other aspect is the effective marketing and promotion of library usage. A library is driven by user needs. At the same time, it is a complex entity, and its potential clientele must become aware of the library's resources and services, and often, be oriented and trained in how to use those resources and services.

Financial Development

Some small libraries may be fortunate, and never have any concerns regarding adequate funding. For example, a corporate library manager may have an understanding with the firm's management that any book or journal can be purchased up to a specified maximum amount. Even a nonprofit library in a church or social service agency may have a relatively open-ended budget and an ample supply of human resources and space.

The more common situation is that funding is inadequate to purchase even the basic resources, there is insufficient space for the library's collections and users, and sufficient staff are not available to operate the library for more than a limited number of hours. These are problems common to all types and size libraries.

A number of options are available to libraries seeking to supplement their usual source of revenue. These include solicitation of gifts or donations, fees for service, special events, sales of resources and services, and for some types of libraries, the creation of endowments or dedicated funds.

Gifts: Solicitation of gifts and donations is probably the most common fund raising strategy. Many libraries receive books, journals and other resources without even asking. Some libraries also gain volunteers who donate their time, which can be a valuable supplement. However, the best approach the manager can take is to develop a gift and donation policy, and to publicize it widely throughout the parent organization. People should be informed that the library accepts and appreciates gifts and donations, and the conditions of acceptance. This could appear in the parent organization's newsletter, or in the community newspaper. A small flyer distributed at the library information desk would be another approach, and many small libraries have designed attractive materials for this purpose.

Endowments and Bequests: An endowment is a gift provided by an individual donor, firm or organization that provides income for a specified time, and often for a specific purpose. An endowment will often be restricted so that only the interest earned from investing the principle can spent, thereby assuring a continuous source of revenue in the future. Bequests are similar grants cited in an individual's will. Many small libraries of all types derive income from endowments and bequests, and the nonprofit library manager should develop strategies to encourage these gifts.

Again, a policy on the acceptance of endowments and bequests should be developed and publicized, so that individuals are aware of this opportunity. A key factor for some donors is whether the library or its parent organi-

Watch out for these problems with gifts

Care must be taken to avoid problems with gifts. For example, someone may wish to donate funds for the creation of a collection that is inappropriate for the library, and it is strongly recommended that any gift or donation policy contain a clause that clearly states that donations may be refused or referred to other organizations. A letter of appreciation is also an essential courtesy for any gift or donation. However, the library manager should never provide an assessment of value for materials or equipment that may be donated, since an qualified independent appraisal is essential for tax deduction purposes.

zation is classified as a charitable organization. In the U.S. the Internal Revenue Service is responsible for this determination. If the library does not have this designation, consideration should be given in gaining it, since it will allow the library to be eligible for many other types of gifts and grants. It is recommended that legal and accounting assistance be sought in the application for this designation. If it is determined that it might be difficult for the library or its parent organization to gain this designation, another alternative is to create an independent foundation dedicated to support the library.

Fees for Services: While it may be inappropriate for some types of libraries, the establishment of user fees for services or resources is another option. The most common fee is for photocopy service, but some libraries charge for computerized reference service, interlibrary loan, rental of meeting rooms or equipment, and selected types of library materials which may be costly or in high demand.

Considerable care must be taken to ensure that the fees do not hinder access, or become discriminatory or arbitrary. Some cost analysis is also advised to determine whether the fees may cost more to administer and collect than the revenue they generate. Again, an advisory committee of users would be helpful in assessing this option, and in determining a equitable policy and fee schedule.

Special Events: It would be unusual to find a small library of any type that has not benefited from a special event of one kind or another. Special events are fund raisers that may be bake sales, author dinners, used book sales, auctions or raffles. They can be time consuming, but with good organization they can be fun and create good support and awareness for the library.

It is recommended that a volunteer committee be recruited for organizing and implementing a special event. In many situations this is not difficult, and service on such a committee is often a social plum. It is not an ongoing obligation, and many people are willing to make a short term commitment. A key to the success of such an event is a handbook or planning manual which defines the tasks, deadlines, and resources on which the volunteers can draw.

Another key to success is placement of the event in the parent organization's or community's calendar of events to avoid competition with other events. Marketing is especially critical, and the best strategy is to get the volunteers to identify the potential audience, and divide up responsibilities for calling them. A personal contact is infinitely more effective than a mailing. To be successful in generating revenue from any event, every effort should be made to get most of the required elements (i.e., food, printing, space, etc.) donated. Finally, the planning and implementation committee should be urged to establish a fund-raising goal for the event, so they have a target to measure their success, and as an incentive to future committees.

Sale of Resources and Services: On occasion a library may have surplus equipment, resources or other assets which can be used to generate additional revenue. It may also be possible for a library to sell some of its services to another entity. For example, the library may have staff expertise, special collections, and equipment it can make available to other organizations for a negotiated amount. These are all valuable alternatives which the manager may wish to consider if additional revenue is needed.

The Foundation Board
Formation of a foundation requires the recruitment of a board of directors, and many libraries have found that these individuals are often willing to volunteer their time to develop fund raising campaigns, and solicit gifts from firms and individuals.

Fees for service is controversial issue for many tax supported libraries, since it is argued that the fee represents a double tax, and that is particularly discriminatory to children and the poor. Those who favor fees, however, argue that fees permit libraries to offer resources and services that could not be provided using usual revenue sources.

However, if any assets or services are sold, care must be taken to ensure that authority has been given by the parent organization, and that no legal barriers exist. For example, many tax supported libraries must adhere to their governmental jurisdiction's surplus property procedures. Inventory records must be adjusted. Used books and other library materials may have the library's ownership mark on them, and this should either be removed, or the material should be marked as "discarded," otherwise the materials may be returned to the library in error.

Other Financial Options: Foundations and governmental agencies often grant funds to many different types of libraries, and the preparation of grant applications is another source of funds. For example, many state library agencies will award special grants to convert the bibliographic records of the holdings of special libraries to computer format, in return for transmission of those records to the state library's union catalog of library holdings.

However, it should be realized the many of the major foundations receive far more grant requests than they can possibly consider, and that many federal and state programs are being reduced because of economic conditions. Local foundations are usually a better source for grants, and the library manager should consult the *Foundation Directory* (cited in the bibliography at the end of this chapter) for information on local foundations and their goals and requirements. The state library agency and regional cooperative library system are also good resources in learning about available grants and local foundations.

Marketing and Promotion

While many users understand the function of a library today, the library manager should never assume that there is universal awareness of how to use library resources, or that everyone knows what library services and resources exist. This is particularly true of the smaller library which may have specialized collections and services.

In chapter 2 on planning, reference was made of techniques which could provide better insight to user needs, expectations and desired services and resources. While these surveys, interviews, and the use of advisory committees are good strategies to build awareness of library services and resources, they are only part of the answer. Many people do not know about interlibrary loan or specialized computer databases, and these important services could be omitted if the library manager depends only upon user suggestions and requests.

Interviews with small groups of users may allow the manager to determine whether some new equipment or an expansion of an existing service might be well received. Suggestions for new services and materials purchases should also be sought and encouraged. This encourages the library's users to take greater interest in the library and feel they are a part of the service.

Marketing involves the identification of needs, even when the user or potential consumer may be unable to articulate what those needs are. In many respects it eliminates or reduces the need to "sell" or promote a particular service. It requires a sensitivity to both those who use the library, as well as those who might become users if the right resources or services were available.

Advice from The Frugal Librarian

The Frugal Librarian recommends three other ways of generating additional financial resources.

1 Ensure that the library is operating as efficiently as possible. Getting the best price for contractual services may require contacting other suppliers, but competitive bidding can save considerable money. Also, there may be services or equipment the library can do without.

2 Terminate infrequently used services, or end the purchase of infrequently used types of materials, and reallocate those savings to support other services.

3 Approach the library's supervisor, governance, or go directly to the users, depending on the nature of the library and its parent organization, to communicate the need for a larger budget to support expansion, new equipment or staff, or more resources. Building a case for this increase necessitates careful research and good justification, but this may be the most practical alternative, particularly if it can be demonstrated that the library is run efficiently, and that usage is growing.

While marketing techniques use research to determine need, they do not eliminate the need to promote greater awareness of the library, and to communicate the availability of those resources and services to all the library's potential users.

There are a number of promotional techniques and strategies the library manager should consider, and they include newsletters, special brochures, effective signage, tours, exhibits and displays, promotional events, and most important of all, personal contact.

Publications

Every library should have a user's guide that summarizes mission, services, collections, hours of service and any pertinent policies relating to the user's obligations. It is the library's primary promotional piece, and it can save time and avoid misunderstanding. In the informal setting of many small libraries, it is often taken for granted that users are aware of this information, when in fact they may not.

Another basic publication for many small libraries is a listing of the subscriptions received, and if possible, a description of the length of time these publications are retained. Depending on the size of the library and its complexity, a simple map of the location of major collections or sections may also be desirable.

Some libraries generate descriptive brochures of special collections or resources, and this can be very helpful in promotion and building usage. However, care is needed to ensure that the library does not generate so many special brochures that they clutter the information or circulation desk. If they are developed, they should be well written and attractively designed so they do not create a negative impression about the library. On occasion the manager may purchase some new special resource that may come with an attractive descriptive brochure produced by the publisher or manufacturer. With the permission of the seller, the manager might consider reproducing this brochure and circulating it to potential users.

Some libraries have developed newsletters which allow them to inform users of new acquisitions, services or changes which will promote greater use of the library. If the library is part of a parent organization that has a newsletter for reaching users or employees, the manager might consider developing a regular column for this communication.

Signage

Every library should have effective signage to aid users. It is often neglected in small libraries, or if signage is used, it may be poorly designed. Some libraries use hand-lettered posters and stenciled directional signs, along with flyers of events, over so many surfaces that the library begins to look like a country store. This visual pollution becomes so bad that users do not see the key signs, and they may gain an impression that the library is cluttered and unorganized.

Signage should be professionally prepared and used sparingly. Most library suppliers offer standard signs and proper mounting devices in their catalogs, and some will also offer custom sign making services so that the signage will be uniform in style and easier for users to see.

The Frugal Librarian strongly suggests that the library manager keep current with new resources and services emerging in the field, and test these, whenever possible, upon selected users. For example, many publishers will loan specialized reference tools, or provide sample journals, upon request. These can be circulated to pertinent users in the organization to gain their assessment.

The Frugal Librarian advises that signage be used sparingly. However, frequent requests for certain types of resources or services are good indication that some signage may be needed.

Type face selected for signage should be clear and large enough to read from a distance. Wording should be brief, and pictographs should be considered if they are available.

Basic signage for a small library should consist of the library's name and hours of operation, to be mounted near the entrance. If the hours vary, signage should be selected which allows easy substitution so hand printed attachments are not needed. A large sign is also needed to identify where users may go in the library for assistance. Even a small library may have several service desks, and it is important to direct the user to the correct location. If there are different sections of the library, such as children's books, periodicals, or reference books, signage should identify these. Classification codes are also very useful on the shelving end panels. Rest rooms and conference rooms need to be clearly marked. Local regulations will also require exit signs, and handicapped accessibility signage.

Official notices and announcements of important events, as well as other public relations materials provided by other organizations should be placed on a bulletin board in a prominent place in the library. Every library receives requests for promoting these events, and the library will usually have notices of its own. The bulletin board should be weeded regularly, and policies should be established that maintain some control over what is posted, and by whom.

Tours

If the library is part of a larger organization, the manager has other opportunities to promote awareness. Most organizations have orientations for new employees, and the user brochure would be a valuable item for distribution at that time. Incidently, the library manager should also ensure that a tour of the library and an explanation of its services is part of the orientation. Visitors are often given a tour of many institutions such as corporations, hospitals, museums and churches. Again, if the library is part of such a parent organization, the library manager should see that the library is included.

Exhibits and Displays

It is essential that every library have some exhibit and display space. Even a small library should reserve some wall or floor space for this purpose because it will be so useful in promoting awareness of new resources and services. Bulletin boards are one basic resource, and the library manager can use book jackets or special mounting devices to publicize new materials. Many publishers distribute colorful posters, and most library supply catalogs feature attractive posters, display cases and stands.

A floor or window display is highly desirable in attracting user attention, and can become a very valuable educational and marketing resource for the library. Both cases and bulletin boards need to be lighted if possible, and cases should be lockable to ensure that users do not become tempted to prematurely borrow display materials.

Events

There are numerous opportunities for the library to piggyback on events, or even to initiate its own events to promote greater awareness among its users.

John Cotton Dana Awards

The American Library Association's Library Administration and Management Association (LAMA) annually sponsors a competition known as the John Cotton Dana Awards, and this is designed to recognize outstanding library marketing and promotion activities. All types and sizes of libraries are eligible, and the winners are displayed at the ALA Annual Conference. The ALA also publishes summaries of the winning programs, and these might be useful in gaining promotional and marketing ideas.

In April of each year the American Library Association, with the aid of the Advertising Council and other major sponsors, widely promotes National Library Week. Public service announcements appear on radio and television, and many newspapers and magazines contain ads. Many suppliers offer kits that can be used in small libraries to benefit from this national campaign.

There is also National Children's Book Week in November, Black History Month in February, birthdays of famous authors, and of course, the holidays, which can offer good opportunity to colorful displays. Special libraries can piggyback on Law Day, Secretary's Week, Dental Health Week, and the multitude of special events which exist. *Chase's Calendar of Events* and *The Librarian's Engagement Calendar* (cited in the bibliography at the end of this chapter) are useful resources in identifying these dates. Appendix F to this book also contains a basic calendar of promotional events that will be useful to any small library.

Further Resources

Chase's Calendar of Events. Lincolnwood, IL: NTC/Contemporary, annual.

Crotz, D. Keith. *Used Book Sales: Less Work & Better Profits.* Ft. Atkinson, WI: Highsmith Press, 1995. 80p.

Foundation Center Staff. *National Guide to Funding for Libraries & Information Services,* 4th ed. New York: Foundation Center, 1997. 234p.

Herring, Mark Y. *Organizing Friends Groups.* New York: Neal-Schuman, 1992. 200p.

Kies, Cosette. *Marketing & Public Relations for Libraries.* Metuchen, NJ: Scarecrow, 1987. 214p.

Kohn, Rita and Tepper, Krysta A. *Have You Got What They Want? Public Relations Strategies for the School Librarian-Media Specialist: A Reference Tool,* 2nd ed. Metuchen, NJ: Scarecrow, 1990. 245p.

Leerburger, Benedict A. *Promoting & Marketing the Library,* rev. ed. New York: Macmillan, 1989. 300p.

Librarian's Engagement Calendar. Ft. Atkinson, WI: Highsmith Press, annual.

Liebold, Louise C. *Fireworks, Brass Bands & Elephants: Promotional Events with Flair for Libraries & Other Nonprofit Organizations.* Phoenix, AZ: Oryx Press, 1986. 144p.

Menard, Christine. *More Bright and Bold Bulletin Boards.* Ft. Atkinson, WI: Alleyside Press, 1995. 64p.

Rounds, Richard. *Basic Budgeting Practices for Librarians.* 2nd ed. Chicago: ALA, 1994. 159p.

Sherman, Steve. *ABCs of Library Promotion,* 3rd ed. Lanham, MD: Scarecrow Press, 1992. 262p.

Steele, Victoria, and Stephen D. Elder. *Becoming a Fundraiser: The Principles and Practice of Library Development.* 2nd ed. Chicago: ALA, 2000. 184p.

Swan, James. *Fundraising for the Small Public Library.* New York: Neal-Schuman, 1990. 238p.

Tedeschi, Anne C. *Book Displays: A Library Handbook.* Ft. Atkinson, WI: Highsmith Press, 1996. 120p.

Walters, Suzanne. *Marketing: A How-to-Do-It Manual for Librarians.* New York: Neal-Schuman, 1992. 103p.

Warner, Alice. *Making Money: Fees for Library Services.* New York: Neal-Schuman, 1989. 150p.

Weingand, Darlene E. *Future-Driven Library Marketing.* Chicago: ALA, 1998. 190p.

Don't Overlook the Importance of Personal Contact

While promotion and market research are vital to building usage, the library manager should not neglect personal contact. Every effort should be made to keep in touch with user needs, and the manager should stress the importance of pleasant contact and a service attitude with all the library's staff and volunteers

Advice from The Frugal Librarian

Consider collecting the e-mail addresses of the library's users, and save postage by e-mailing your library newsletter, promotional announcements, and overdue reminders. If you use a registration card to obtain borrower information, it would be well to explain why you are requesting the user's e-mail address, to ensure the individual doesn't object. However, most persons are used to being asked for their e-mail address, for they are aware of the convenience of e-mail. As long as you respect the user's privacy, and don't sell or give the information to a third party, you shouldn't experience any problems.

Small Public Libraries

Chapter 12

The Mission and Objectives of the Public Library

Public libraries generally have the broadest user base of any type of library, for virtually any resident of their service area, from a toddler to a university professor, may have access to their collections and services. While the primary mission of these libraries is to serve the residents of a specific community or political jurisdiction, state or provincial law, or contractual or cooperative agreements may extend their services to other jurisdictions. In addition, the public library has the responsibility of serving the present and future needs of its clientele, and that necessitates building a collection and designing services that are appropriate to those needs.

The number of public libraries is steadily increasing throughout the world, from China to Africa, because of the growing importance of education and information to economic development. There are over 9,000 public libraries in the United States. Some are quite large, with numerous branch libraries and bookmobiles. The vast majority, however, serve 5,000 or fewer persons, operate from a single building, and have collections and budgets which are commensurate in size. While there may be a variety of goals and objectives cited in the laws and regulations governing these institutions, their most common objectives include learning community needs, usually through a planning process and community study, and the design and creation of collections and services that are responsive to those needs. That necessitates an evaluation based on measurement of use. However, the local governance of each library generally has the greatest role and responsibility for defining specific goals and objectives.

Other public library goals include supplementing the collections of other libraries such as schools and colleges in fostering basic and higher education, providing for the continuing education of adults, cultural enrichment, economic development and recreation.

Governance and Relationship to Local Government

State and provincial law dictates which political jurisdictions may create a local public library. In the U.S., approximately 50 percent of all public libraries are municipal departments, and 25 percent are county libraries. The balance are jurisdictions such as townships, school districts and villages. There are also a growing number of independent library districts which were established for the sole purpose of supplying library services to a defined geographic area.

In all but a few states, U.S. public libraries are legally governed by a board of trustees that may be appointed by a designated official such as the mayor or county executive, and confirmed by a city council or county board of supervisors. Some libraries, such as many independent library districts, may have elected boards. Trustees usually serve without pay, and they are charged with the selection and supervision of a library manager or director, creation of policies governing library service, development of a budget, and the planning and evaluation of service. Trustees vary in number, but often there are five to twelve persons on a board. Because they are volunteers, boards delegate authority to the library manager for daily operation of the institution, under the board's policies. The powers and duties of the library's board of trustees are usually prescribed by state law and local statutes.

However, some libraries do not have a board of trustees, and the library manager may report directly to a city, county or village manager or some other official who may be elected or appointed. In that situation, there may be an advisory board of citizens who are appointed by the governing authority to provide input on services and policies. In actual practice, library managers may find that they have obligations to a board, appointed officials such as a city manager, and to various elected officials such as a mayor and city council. This is due to the shared nature of certain responsibilities such as development and approval of a budget, and the need to ensure communication between all levels of government. Some boards may have elected not to exercise some of the powers granted to them by law, or they may have surrendered some of their powers at the request of an appointed official. This can create some confusion, particularly if the state has home rule provisions. Under home rule, the local political jurisdiction is assumed to have all powers not specifically reserved by the state or federal government.

Public Library Policies and Procedures

Public libraries usually have the power to create rules and regulations regarding usage, and they are also subject to local ordinances, administrative policies and procedures created by their political jurisdictions. For example, failure to return overdue library materials, destruction of library property, creating a disturbance in the reading rooms are typical infractions of public library rules, and most libraries prescribe some form of penalty such as loss of library borrowing privileges for repeated offenses. Some of these rules have the force of law, meaning that the library may have the right to take someone to court to resolve a problem associated with them.

As a result, public libraries typically have a handbook containing their policies for referral and training. These policies may be public service or administrative in nature, and there may also be procedures which describe how the policies are to be implemented or administered. Public service policies may include hours of service, loan periods, borrower eligibility and similar matters. The source of the policy and its effective date should be cited for reference in case some question arises. Administrative policies will include personnel rules, purchasing requirements, book selection policies, surplus property disposal, and the host of other regulations under which the library operates. Again, the source of the policy and its effective date are important in the event someone should question its validity.

Monthly Board Meetings

Typically, it is the role of the library manager to plan the board's regular meeting agenda with the board's president or chairperson. The agenda should include reports on usage, finance, personnel and planning; and recommendations for new or revised programs and policies. Many boards also have committees for certain matters such as finance and administration.

Every library manager should have a solid understanding of these policies and procedures, and be able to interpret them as questions or problems arise, either with the public or staff. While these policies are important to ensure consistency and fairness in dealing with the public and staff, and vital for training staff, they can become a public relations problem if they are interpreted without flexibility. Moreover, the library manager needs to be sensitive to policies or procedures which are the source of friction, and be ready to recommend amendment or deletion to the board or appropriate official. Several books are cited at the end of this chapter which contain standard or recommended policies. Other libraries may be willing to lend their policies and procedures manuals for comparison. It is also recommended the policy and procedures manuals be kept as concise and simple as possible.

Public Library Finance

Most public libraries are dependent upon the local property tax as their primary source of revenue. Some states allocate funds to local libraries, or there may be a special or dedicated tax for libraries. Endowments, fees, contracts and special grants are other typical sources. The library manager is usually responsible for recommending an annual budget for approval by the library board, who in turn forward the budget with any appropriate amendments to the local appropriating authority. Following review, the budgeting authority will incorporate the library's budget in its own operating budget, which is derived from the broader revenue sources available to the jurisdiction. This is likely to include property taxes, state or provincial grants, fees and contracts, and other miscellaneous revenues. Various budgeting techniques were cited in previous chapters, and they won't be repeated here. However, it is important to remember that the annual budget should always be developed in relation to the library's long range plan.

Many public jurisdictions have a capital budget as will as an operating budget. Capital budgets are typically developed for physical construction, expansion or major maintenance, and often they are treated as if they are entirely separate from the operating budget. In some instances jurisdictions may consider the book budget or other major equipment such as a computer to be capital expenditures. Some jurisdictions support capital expenditures out of ongoing tax revenues; some issue bonds or require public referenda for their approval.

While the library manager may have the primary responsibility for developing the annual operating or capital improvements budget, it is important that the manager confer with the political jurisdiction's budget officer in advance to learn the preferred form of submission and justification, and to identify any perimeters or goals. Most jurisdictions have budget targets, and it is well to know these as early as possible. The library board may elect to ignore these if they believe the library has unique and special needs, such as a badly needed repair or a new service, but the library manager must inform them of the recommended guidelines. When the time comes for the library's budget request to be considered by the budgeting authority, it is also advisable that it be presented by the library board's president or representative, since the board is the best advocate for that budget. The library manager can be a resource to respond to any technical questions.

Searching for extra funds for your library could become a full-time activity, and some boards and governing officials have unreasonable expectations on this matter. The Frugal Librarian suggests that this subject be thoroughly discussed with the library board and local officials. While the library manager has a role in financial development, her primary role is to ensure the library uses its funds efficiently and serves its users well. Statistics show that taxes constitute 90–95 percent of public library revenues, and if boards and officials expect to attract revenues from other sources, they will need to either invest their time in the effort or recruit other volunteers.

Legal Requirements

Even under home rule, local jurisdictions can only create public libraries if state or provincial law permits it. There may be other requirements imposed under the law, such as the filing of an annual statistical and financial report. As a result, the state exercises a degree of control and often imposes certain obligations. This is particularly evident if the state furnishes any financial aid to the local library. Accordingly, every library manager should become familiar with state and provincial library law. Most state library agencies have compiled summaries of these laws and other regulations, and they can be obtained through a letter or phone call. The purpose of these state library agencies is to aid in the development of local library service, and to encourage resource sharing. A complete list of all state and provincial library agencies is contained in appendix A of this book.

Some states have requirements governing the qualifications of public library administrators. This may consist of minimal training or experience. Formal application may be required to gain certification, and the state may require the manager to attend classes or conferences at regular intervals to maintain knowledge of trends in the library field. Again, the state library agency can provide information on certification requirements, and assist the manager in obtaining and maintaining eligibility.

The library manager also needs to establish a good relationship with the political jurisdiction's legal counsel. Often there is a city attorney or county corporation counsel who officially represents the library and can render opinions on the law and its application to the library. In some instances, the library board may have a trustee who is an attorney, and he or she may be able to provide informal assistance. However, care should be taken to avoid a conflict of interest, which may occur if the attorney-trustee renders a legal opinion affecting his/her powers or role on the board.

Typical Services and Organizational Structure

Many public libraries divide collections and services into adult and youth divisions because of the different needs of these age levels, and it is often customary to have a children's specialist. Adult services often include a specialist who is able to provide reference and referral services, and perhaps offer some reader's advisory assistance to more specialized literature. It is also common to have a circulation or lending function, and a technical processing operation, depending on the availability of staff. Circulation staff would administer materials lending policies and procedures, borrower registration, take reservations for selected titles, and be responsible for shelving. Technical processing functions would include ordering, cataloging and classification, processing and mending, as well as general collection maintenance. Interlibrary loan could be handled by any of these positions. There is also the administrative and building maintenance responsibilities. Some larger libraries may also have outreach specialists if they have branches, bookmobiles or other types of extension such as book deposit stations, books by mail or services to special groups such as the home bound.

Of course, in the one person library, all of these responsibilities will fall on the single individual, unless volunteers are recruited (which is highly rec-

Advice from The Frugal Librarian

If the library does not already have a friends group, the Frugal Librarian strongly recommends the manager gain the approval and assistance of the library board and officials in starting a Friends of the Library. Advice can be obtained in the U.S. from Friends of Libraries USA (FOLUSA), an affiliate of the ALA (1420 Walnut St., Ste. 450, Philadelphia, PA 19103. Tel: 215/790-1674; Fax: 215/545-3821; E-mail: folusa@libertynet.org; Web: www.folusa.com). These volunteers can promote the library, solicit gifts, and become a welcome source of ideas.

ommended). As the public library grows in usage and funding, it is more customary for a simple hierarchy to be created. In this organizational setting the library manager reports to the library board or other governing authority, and all staff in turn report to the manager. As staffing and scheduling grows more complicated, supervisory responsibility is delegated to those who have supportive staff. A good example is the circulation supervisor. Typically, students are hired on a part-time basis to aid in shelving materials returned by borrowers. These part-time staff are often under the direction of the circulation supervisor, who trains and schedules this staff.

While this is a typical list of services and organizational structure, it is not universal. Some cooperative library system services or contractual arrangement may exist that would allow a small library to offer other varied services. It all depends on the creativity of the library manager and the library board.

Resources

Associations

The best source of information on public library service in the U.S. is the Public Library Association (PLA), a division of the American Library Association (50 E. Huron Street, Chicago, IL 60611, 312-280-5752, Fax 312-280-5029). A majority of the members of this division are persons employed in small and medium-sized public libraries, and the association offers publications, conferences and training opportunities. PLA publishes *Public Libraries*, a bi-monthly journal.

The American Library Trustees Association is another division of the ALA relating to public libraries. It is located at the same address, and its telephone number is 312-280-2161. This organization can provide assistance to trustees who may have questions or concerns, and it offers publications and programs designed to keep trustees current.

Books

Cassell, Kay, and Elizabeth Futas. ***Developing Public Library Collections, Policies, and Procedures.*** New York: Neal-Schuman, 1991. 143p.

Fasick, Adele M. ***Managing Children's Services in the Public Library,*** 2nd ed. Englewood, CO: Libraries Unlimited, 1998. 218p.

Gertzog, Alice, and Edwin Beckerman. ***Administration of the Public Library.*** Lanham, MD: Scarecrow Press, 1994. 601p.

Hall, Richard. ***Financing Public Library Buildings.*** New York: Neal-Schuman, 1994. 299p.

Hayes, Robert, and Virginia Walter. ***Strategic Management for Public Libraries: A Handbook.*** Westport, CT: Greenwood, 1996. 248p.

Larson, Jeanette, and Herman Totten. ***Model Policies for Small & Medium Public Libraries.*** New York: Neal-Schuman, 1998. 214p.

McClure, Charles, et al. ***Planning and Role Setting for Public Libraries: A Manual of Procedures.*** Chicago, ALA, 1987. 117p.

Reed, Sally. ***Small Libraries: A Handbook for Successful Management.*** Jefferson, NC: McFarland, 1991. 156p.

Weingand, Darlene E. ***Administration of the Small Public Library,*** 3rd ed. Chicago: ALA, 1992. 138p.

Woodrum, Patricia, and Sul Lee. ***Managing Public Libraries in the 21st Century.*** Binghamton, NY: Haworth Press, 1989. 232 p.

Young, Virginia. ***The Library Trustee: A Practical Guidebook,*** 5th ed. Chicago: ALA, 1995. 240 p.

Associations for Libraries Beyond the U.S.

The library associations in other nations such as Canada and the United Kingdom also have divisions devoted to public library service. A comprehensive listing of these associations can be found in the *International Literary Market Place* (Bowker, annual). State and provincial library associations are also excellent resources, and most have divisions devoted to public library concerns and issues. Your state or provincial library agency can provide information on these associations. There is also a comprehensive listing in *The Bowker Annual Library and Book Trade Almanac* (Bowker, annual).

Small School Libraries & Media Centers

Chapter 13

School libraries and media centers are an essential component of the educational system. Although historical records indicate they have existed for hundreds of years in schools throughout the world, no precise date can be cited when the first school library was established. In colonial America, evidence exists that Benjamin Franklin recommended the development of a school library in the design of a model academy for students in 1740. Many schools maintained collections of texts and other books for student and faculty use, but it was not until 1835 that New York State enacted legislation officially permitting school districts to purchase library books.

Although many recognized the importance of access to good books in the school, the formal development of the school library was slow and deliberate. The first census of libraries in the U.S. conducted by the federal government in 1876 recorded the existence of only 826 high school libraries in the entire nation. Formation of a library section by the National Education Association in 1896 and a school library section by the ALA in 1914 led to a joint effort to create standards for secondary schools. This was followed by standards for elementary school libraries in 1925. While these were useful, the Great Depression and World War II slowed their acceptance and application. It was not until the end of World War II that the first comprehensive standards were developed and adopted by the ALA, to be subsequently followed by other revisions to aid school librarians and administrators in the design and operation of the modern school library media program.

Today the school library may be known as the instructional media center, educational resource center, learning resources center or some variation, but whatever the name, it is a valued and vital component of the school, essential to the curriculum.

The Role and Responsibilities of the School Library/Media Center

Just as every library needs a mission statement as a basis for long range planning, each school library media center needs to develop a statement that is in keeping the needs of the school and community. It is generally believed that the purpose of the school media center is to aid in the fulfillment of the instructional goals and objectives of the school and to promote these goals through the selection and organization of educational resources such as books and audiovisual materials, as well as to ensure that students are given access and instruction on the use of these resources. Beyond this generalized view, the school library media center manager needs to refine that statement so that it may serve as a benchmark for more specific planning.

To aid in the development of this mission statement and plan, the manager should consider the creation of an advisory committee that is representative of the various users or constituents of the media center. That should include the students, faculty, school administration, and preferably the parents. Besides offering valuable input, the advisory committee can also become an advocate for the center during budgeting. The other steps described in chapter 2 on planning can also be applied in the development of an appropriate plan for organization, operation and development

Relationship to School Administration and Faculty

The key policy making body for every school system is the school board, and ultimately the school library media center must operate within those policies. Even private schools will have some board to establish policies, evaluate the chief administrator's performance and approve a budget. While schools are greatly influenced by state and federal legislative mandates in the U.S., and by state boards of education, the local school board still exercises considerable autonomy in prioritization and allocation of financial resources. School members are either elected or appointed, and they have powers, duties and terms decreed by the state.

One of the primary responsibilities of the school board is the selection and supervision of the system chief executive, the school superintendent. While the board has some discretion in terms of requirements and attributes, the state and profession usually impose some minimum requirements. Once selected, the superintendent operates through an administrative staff who are delegated responsibilities for key sections of the system such as curriculum and instruction. One of these administrators may have responsibility for school library media programs, and the manager may be selected and report to that person. However, many school systems have teachers and librarians selected by the school principal. In some instances, selection and reporting responsibilities may be shared to various degrees between the superintendent or an administrative officer, the district personnel office, and the school principal.

It is therefore imperative that the school library media center manager know the school district's organizational structure, and gains a clear understanding of reporting responsibilities. Another important key step is building rapport with the faculty, and to do this requires an understanding of the curriculum and the needs of each teacher. Discussion with each faculty member will provide a starting point, and study of their lesson plans and schedules will be of further value. While every system follows a uniform curriculum and schedule, some variation is inevitable, and the center manager needs to be sensitive to these differences.

Advice from The Frugal Librarian

Courses in school librarianship are offered by many colleges and universities specializing in teacher training. The Frugal Librarian also suggests consideration be given to "distance learning" programs, especially if you're in an area which does not have a college offering these courses. Distance learning is offered by a number of universities via satellite and videotaped lectures. Students can earn credits toward certification. Schools offering these courses include the University of Arizona, Clarion State University, among many others. Information can be obtained from the Library and Information Science Distance Education Consortium (Dr. Daniel Barron, University of South Carolina, College of Library and Information Science, Columbia, SC 29208, 803/ 777-3858).

Legal Requirements

The individual responsible for the school library media center may have one of various titles, such as media specialist, school library media specialist, or school librarian. However, in the U.S. the position often requires certification, usually by the state's department of education. Some states allow temporary certification, but when this occurs it is assumed the individual will seek to satisfy the normal requirements of the position as soon as possible. To gain this certification, the individual must complete a course of study at an accredited undergraduate or graduate university or college. Degrees as a school library media specialist can be earned at either the undergraduate or graduate level, and they are offered in schools of education and schools of library and information science. There may be different levels and types of certification required for different schools, such as for high schools and elementary schools. States differ in their requirements for certification, and individuals should contact their state department of education to determine the courses and number of hours of instruction that are required.

The curriculum of local school systems is also affected by the state, which may establish a minimum number of hours of instruction in specific subjects, such as history or physical education. These are translated by each district into instructional units, and the school library media specialist needs to be sensitive to these requirements in the development of the collection.

In addition, in the U.S. the state department of education may have some minimum standards or requirements for school library media centers, such as collection size, staffing or funding. It is the primary responsibility of the school superintendent to ensure that the school system is in compliance with these regulations. However, this may be delegated to other school administrative staff, and it is also important that the media specialist provide assistance in meeting these requirements.

While many professional associations may have standards they recommend for library media centers and programs, they do not have the force of law, and are only desirable recommendations until they are adopted by the state. There may be a considerable difference between standards and requirements because of the reluctance of state officials to mandate improvements that would require increases in local or state taxes. Accordingly, the library media specialist is often interpreting standards for administrative staff and faculty, and seeking to convert these into reality through the budget process.

School Library Budgeting

While the school board and superintendent has ultimate responsibility for the development of the system's annual budget, some responsibilities may be delegated to principals or staff at the building level. Earlier chapters on administration and finance apply in aiding the school media center specialist to prepare a budget recommendation. While standards are of great value in the development and evaluation of budget requests, it should be recognized that they have some limitations when they are viewed by administrators who may be confronted by recommended standards from other educational professions and legal mandates, at the same time they might be experiencing either public resistance to increased taxes or erosion of the local tax base.

Accordingly, the media specialist needs to temper budget requests with the reality of current economic conditions, and learn to carefully justify increases. Strengthening the media center collection will certainly make a contribution to many of the system's curriculum goals, and these need to be cited. Changes in the curriculum will also justify purchase new equipment or resources. Growing usage may also justify additional staff or materials. The media specialist also needs to notify administrators of potential savings. For example, participation in a cooperative multitype library system may grant access to more resources or other services such as system delivery.

With the exception of private schools, most public schools are dependent on revenues from the local property tax, supplemented by varying amounts of state and federal grants. Some states use a formula for allocation of these funds based on student enrollment or other elements such as the relative wealth of the local tax base. The formula may also include some amount for maintenance of school library media centers. The media specialist needs to understand this funding formula, and ensure that the formula is not interpreted in such fashion to be detrimental to the school library media center.

The continuing concern for further improvement in education has also led to the creation of many state and federal aid programs which can be of direct or indirect benefit to the media center. Many foundations and corporations are taking greater interest in education, and this could result in grants which might be appropriate for the media center. State and national professional associations, as well as state library agencies can provide information on grant opportunities. There are other alternative revenue possibilities cited in chapter 11, which merit consideration by the media specialist.

Advice from the Frugal Librarian

If advocacy in gaining adequate financial support for a school library is needed, the Frugal Librarian recommends that an advisory committee, friends group or the Parent Teacher Association may be most appropriate. They're also a source of volunteer assistance and donations. Friends groups have helped many public libraries, and they can be equally effective for school libraries. Contact the Friends of Libraries USA (see their address and telephone numbers in chapter 12) for information.

School Library Policies and Activities

One of the primary distinguishing features of the school library media center is its developmental role in aiding students to learn library research procedures and library resources. More than anything else, the media specialist is a teacher. The emphasis upon the school library as an instructional materials center is to counter the impression among some faculty, students and parents that the library is a study hall or detention center. In some systems students may be disciplined by requiring them to read a specified number of library books, or perform specified library research in penance for their infraction. If the media specialist encounters such policies, every effort is needed to work with faculty and the administration to alter the practice.

Regular contact with the faculty and administration to keep them informed of the center's instructional role is essential. The media specialist can also apply some of the marketing techniques suggested in chapter 11. Working effectively with faculty and the administration, the media specialist can go far in building student appreciation of library service, and strengthen their likelihood of success as they pursue their education.

Work With Other Area Libraries

Cooperation with other libraries in the area will also be helpful in enriching the student's library experience. For example, many public libraries sponsor summer reading programs to maintain reading levels. The school media specialist should work in cooperation with the children's librarians in the public library to make students aware of the program, and to ensure they are issued borrowers' cards.

Resources

Associations

The primary national professional association for media specialists in the U.S. is the American Association of School Librarians, a division of the American Library Association (50 E. Huron St, Chicago, IL 60611, 312-280-4386, Fax 312-664-7459). They sponsor conferences, publications and continuing educational opportunities for an individual associated with school media centers. The Association for Library Service to Children and the Young Adult Library Services Association are two other divisions of the ALA which offer activities and resources for those serving pertinent age level students. In addition, there are state library and media associations with active programs which will greatly benefit media center staff.

Most library associations in other nations also have divisions or affiliated associations devoted to school library service. For example, in the United Kingdom the School Library Association (Liden Library, Barrington Close, Liden, Swinden, Wiltshire SN3 6HF) would be a primary resource. Check the *International Literary Market Place* (Bowker, annual) for a comprehensive listing of these organizations.

Books

American Association of School Librarians and Association for Educational Communications and Technology. *Information Power: Building Partnerships for Learning.* Chicago: ALA, 1998. 224p.

American Association of School Librarians and Association for Educational Communications and Technology. *Information Literacy Standards for Student Learning.* Chicago: ALA, 1998. 64p.

Childress, Valerie. *Winning Friends for the School Library: A PR Handbook.* Worthington, OH: Linworth, 1993. 194p.

Day, Teresa, et al. *Automation for School Libraries: How to Do It from Those Who Have Done It.* Chicago: ALA, 1994. 138p.

Hart, Thomas. *Creative Ideas for Library Media Center Facilities.* Englewood, CO: Libraries Unlimited, 1990. 74p.

Haycock, Ken. *Foundations for Effective School Library Media Programs.* Englewood, CO: Libraries Unlimited, 1999. 331p.

Loertscher, David, and Blanche Woolls. *Information Literacy: A Review of the Research.* San Jose, CA: Hi Willow, 1999. 129p.

Pearson, Richard C. with Kaye Turner. *The School Library Media Specialist's Tool Kit.* Ft. Atkinson: WI: Highsmith Press, 1999. 100p. A concise guide with practical solutions to the most significant challenges facing school librarians.

Rudin, Claire. *The School Librarian's Sourcebook.* New York: R. R. Bowker, 1990. 504p. This is a comprehensive annotated listing of resources of value to media specialists.

Smith, Jane Bandy. *Achieving a Curriculum-Based Library Media Center Program: The Middle School Model for Change.* Chicago: ALA, 1995. 125p.

Van Orden, Phyllis. *Selecting Books for the Elementary School Library Media Center: A Complete Guide.* New York: Neal-Schuman, 2000. 200p.

Wasman, Ann M. *New Steps to Service: Common-Sense Advice for the Library Media Specialist.* Chicago: ALA, 1998. 256p.

Woolls, Blanche. *School Library Media Manager.* 2nd ed. Englewood, CO: Libraries Unlimited, 1999. 340p.

Information Power

In 1998 the American Association of School Librarians (AASL, a division of the ALA), and the Association for Educational Communications and Technology (AECT) jointly published *Information Power: Building Partnerships for Learning* (ALA, 1998, 224p.). Consisting of three categories and nine standards intended to improve information literacy among students, the publication is having a profound impact on school library service. The standards are available at the AASL website (www.ala.org/ aasl.html).

In summarizing these new standards, they are divided into three categories: *Information Literacy, Independent Learning,* and *Society Responsibility,* with three standards listed under each category. The emphasis in the three standards listed under Information Literacy is on how students access, evaluate and use information. The second category, Independent Learning, focuses on how students can search for information, strengthen their appreciation of literature, and strive for excellence. The third category, Social Responsibility, focuses on the importance of information in our democratic society, the ethical responsibilities students should assume in drawing upon technology-related resources, and group use of these resources.

Special Libraries

Chapter 14

We live in a rapidly changing world where information is the most valuable commodity, and education is recognized as the essential path to economic success. Because of the role of libraries in making information accessible and providing resources necessary for continuing education, virtually every type of institution, firm or organization has developed some form of special library today to support its activities. There is a constant need for facts, figures, regulations, procedures, and other data. While the computer has provided the means to organize and access information that many individuals require in their work and everyday life, it has also spawned a requirement for its own supportive reference library. Computer instructional and reference books now comprise a major section in most book stores and public libraries. While some have predicted the demise of the library as technology advances and educational levels rise, there is a much greater likelihood that libraries will continue to increase in number and in specialization.

Because of the difficulty of providing details on every type of special library, this brief guide has concentrated on the major functions common to all types of library, such as the need for planning, organizing the collection, acquiring resources, and methods for serving users. However, there are several types of special libraries where unique issues and resources exist, and these will be summarized in this chapter. Resources that offer more information are suggested in each section.

Church and Synagogue Libraries

The mission of most church and synagogue libraries is to support the work and values of the parent institution. That can be a considerable undertaking, given the activities and challenges facing churches and synagogues today. Certainly the ministry requires research and reference materials for sermons, teaching and other types of formal presentations. In addition, the music ministry will need scores and libretti, hymnals and recordings to ensure this program can be fulfilled. It is also quite likely that these requirements will go beyond the traditional church repertoire to include classical, jazz, folk and other secular works.

The youth program will almost certainly require literature that stresses the teaching and values of the denomination. That also applies to the inspirational works that are available to adult members of the congregation. Many churches and synagogues also have active counseling programs to meet needs such as substance abuse, outreach to the incarcerated, child and elder abuse, and a wide array of social concerns. Unlike the public and school library, the typical church and synagogue library is not necessarily seeking a balanced view. While they are most certainly likely to have materials which reflect diverse opinions on many topics, the church and synagogue collection can and usually does have a point of view.

There are estimated to be over 40,000 church and synagogue libraries in the United States, and there is likely to be considerable variety in their governance and organization. The library manager may report to directly to the pastor or rabbi, to the church or synagogue governing board, or perhaps to a committee appointed by one of those individuals or entities. It is also likely that the library may have a volunteer support staff, given the tradition of volunteerism that is so important a component in the church. Another difference the library manager will notice is the reliance on church publishing houses for library resources. Each of the major denominations have strong publishing programs, and there are a host of independent publishers that specialize in religion. This does not imply that church and synagogue libraries purchase only from these sources. There will always be need for standard reference tools and other secular works in the good church or synagogue library.

Some libraries rely upon a special classification or filing system for organizing the collection. However, this is not recommended because of the reasons which were stated earlier in this text. It is much more advisable to adhere to standard classification and cataloging standards to avoid time consuming processing work, and the library's users will also appreciate a system with which they are familiar.

Books

Church & Synagogue Library Association Staff. *Standards for Church & Synagogue Libraries: Guidelines for Measuring Effectiveness & Progress*. 2nd rev. ed. Portland, OR: Church & Synagogue Library Association, 1993. 24p.

Deitrick, Bernard. *A Basic Book List for Church Libraries*, 5th rev. ed. Portland, OR: Church and Synagogue Library Association, 1995. 17p.

Hannaford, Claudia. *The ABC's of Financing Church & Synagogue Libraries*. Portland, OR: Church and Synagogue Library Association, 1985. 36p.

McMichael, Betty. *The Church Librarian's Handbook*, 3rd rev. ed. Grand Rapids, MI: Baker Books, 1998. 320p.

Smith, Ruth S. *Setting Up a Library: How to Begin or Begin Again*. rev. ed. Portland, OR: Church and Synagogue Library Association, 1994. 20p.

Law Libraries

There are three major types of law libraries in the United States—private, public, and law school. Private law libraries are among the earliest form to be created, and their function is to support the legal research of a relatively limited clientele, such as the partners and associates of a law firm or corporation. Many local or county bar association libraries also fall into this category, since access to the collections may be limited to the membership. Public law libraries have open access, and they often are tax supported. County law libraries are exam-

Associations for Church and Synagogue Libraries

The primary resource for those with responsibility for church and synagogue libraries is the:

Church and Synagogue Library Association
Box 19357
Portland, OR 97280-0357
Tel. 503-244-6919 or toll-free: 800/LIB-CSLA
Fax: 503-977 3734
E-mail: csla@worldaccessnet.com
Web: www.worldasscessnet.com/~csla

They publish an excellent selection of concise and low cost materials of value in organizing and operating this type of special library, including a bi-monthly journal, *Church & Synagogue Libraries.*

Library associations have also been formed for many of the major denominations. Among the largest is the:

Catholic Library Association
C/O SLIS
Dominican University
7900 W Division St.
River Forest, IL 60305-1099
Tel. 708/524-6641
Fax: 708/524-6657

Again, this association offers publications including a quarterly journal (*Catholic Library World*) and an index to Catholic literature.

Others include:
Association of Jewish Libraries
15 E. 26th St. Ste. 1034
New York, NY 10010-1579
Tel. 212/725-5359
Fax: 212/678-8998
Web: aleph.lib.ohio_state.edu/www/ajl/html

Lutheran Church Library Association
122 Franklin Avenue
Minneapolis, MN 55404
Tel. 612/870-3623
Fax: 612/870-0170
E-mail: LCLAHQ@aol.com

Publishes the *Lutheran Librarian* (quarterly)

ples, which are usually open to the general public, but are more frequently heavily used the judges and officers of the court system. A third common type of law library is to be found in an academic institution, where it supports the work of the faculty and provides an essential resource for law students.

Many nations, states, and specialized governmental agencies maintain law libraries to support their legislative, regulatory and judicial responsibilities. Legal collections may also be found in larger public libraries and penal institutions, although they are likely to be of a more general nature.

Development of a sound legal collections requires a knowledge of legal research methodology and the literature. Specialized training in the law and librarianship would be requisite for effective legal library administration. Although it has its critics, the U.S. legal system is considered to be a model, and the existence of a strong network of legal libraries has contributed to this reputation. Because of the nature of American government, collections must be developed containing state laws as well as the federal government. Furthermore, legal research has become so complex that special collections may be required on taxes, family law, criminal law, intellectual property, patents and numerous other branches of law, depending on the nature and needs of the library's clientele.

While resources for law libraries may be purchased from a wide array of legal publishers, state and federal governments are major publishers of legal and regulatory materials which are essential to the operation of a good legal library. Knowledge of governmental publications would be essential to the law library manager. An increasing amount of legal information is available from online databases such as Lexis, and current legislation is also being placed on the Internet, so that insight into these vast resources (see appendix E for information on the Internet) and computer skills are desirable.

Much of the preliminary legal research in large law firms and corporations is conducted by paralegal assistants or junior associate attorneys, often with the assistance of experienced law librarians. Research is also conducted to trace precedents to support the legal positions or arguments placed for consideration before the judiciary. Documenting these precedents, gathering and organizing evidence, drafting legal documents into the correct form and maintenance of the services, collections and records are other responsibilities which often fall upon those associated with various types of law libraries found in the United States.

Books

American Association of Law Librarians Staff & Dyer, Susan. *Manual of Procedures for Private Law Libraries*. Chicago: Am. Assn. of Law Libraries, 1984. 130 p.

American Correctional Association Staff. *Correctional Facilities Law Libraries: An A to Z Resource Guide*. Washington, DC: American Correctional Assn., 1991. 146p.

Dixon, Peter. *The Law Library*. Lantern Books, 1988. 250 p.

Kehoe, Patrick E., et al, eds. *Law Librarianship: A Handbook for the Electronic Age*. Littleton, CO: Rothman, 1995. 640p.

Moys, Elizabeth, ed. *Manual of Law Librarianship: The Use and Organization of Legal Literature*, 2nd ed. New York: Macmillan, 1987. 952p.

Panella, Deborah. *Basics of Law Librarianship*. Binghamton, NY: Haworth, 1991. 136p.

Voges, Mickie. *Building Your Law Library: A Step-by-Step Guide*. Washington, DC: American Bar Association, 1988. 90p.

Associations for Law Libraries

The major resource for those responsible for law libraries in the U.S. is the

American Association of Law Libraries
53 W. Jackson Blvd., Ste. 940
Chicago, IL 60604
Tel. 312/939-4764
Fax: 312/431-1097
E-mail: aallhq@aall.org
Web: www.aallnet.org

This association sponsors conferences, issues publications, offers continuing education opportunities, and supports specialized indexing services.

The American Bar Association
750 N. Lake Shore Dr.
Chicago, IL 60611
Tel. 312/988-5000 or
Toll free: 800/285-2221
Fax: 312/988-5528
is another resource, in addition to the state and local bar associations.

Law library managers in other nations can obtain assistance from the

International Association of Law Libraries
c/o Covington & Burling
1201 Pennsylvania Avenue NW
Washington, DC 20044-7566
Tel. 202/662-6152
Fax: 202/662-6291

Advice from the Frugal Librarian

If the library manager experiences a shortage of resources or the need for a greater variety of materials, the Frugal Librarian recommends that the manager contact the local public library or cooperative library system, since those institutions are likely to have an interest in developing outreach activities to persons who may lack the ability to directly use these libraries.

Business Libraries

The business library is usually defined as the collection and services created for a private corporation or business. While some larger public and academic libraries have special business collections, many industries and corporations, including those engaged in accounting, advertising, banking, consulting, insurance, investment, manufacturing, and publishing, have come to realize the advantages gained by establishing their own special library. The confidentiality of their research may also be a contributing factor to their need for this service. Many nonprofit organizations and government agencies may also have a special collection which might focus on economics or otherwise support the activities of the organization, and this might be referred to as a business library.

Administratively, the business library manager often reports to the chief operating officer or another top position in executive management, since they are the most likely client for the library's services. While business libraries may have traditional book collections, they are more likely to have a rich variety of nonbook materials such as patents, research reports, documents, photographs, and information in other formats, depending on the nature of the corporation's activities. Periodicals and newsletters are another common resource, and these are often routed by the library staff to key personnel to keep them current on trends in the field.

Business library collections are centered on the special services provided by personnel in the corporation and on the industry or field the firm serves. For example, the library in an insurance company will undoubtedly contain materials on computerization, marketing and accounting to serve personnel in those departments, as well as extensive directories and other reference books on the insurance field, insurance regulations from the states where the firm operates. General management, investment and corporate legal resources will have been acquired for top management. The collection may be organized in accordance with a specialized classification and cataloging system, but it is recommended that DDC or LC be used, with modified subject headings if the nature of the collection demands it. Because the typical business library will have a small staff, time for elegant customized organizational schemes will be limited. Moreover, they may be alien to the user.

Specialized reference and research is another service of the business library, and its staff may need to have access to other research collections and online computerized databases in order to conduct this work. Some business libraries index or abstract literature for management, and while this may be appropriate for some fields, there are a growing number of indexes and abstracting services in print and machine readable form that might avoid the necessity for this time consuming activity.

Business libraries tend to have small, but active collections, and the business library manager will have to depend on a network of other libraries or human resources to fulfill its mission. The library manager will also need to develop expertise in the literature of the subject fields in which the corporation is active. If this is lacking, the manager should consider developing a formal or informal advisory committee to assist in developing the collections and special services to support the corporation's activities.

Responsibility for Proprietary Information

Part of the typical business collection is likely to be of a proprietary nature, meaning that it is confidential and essential to the profitability or success of the organization. While business libraries are heavily dependent on interlibrary loan to supplement their special collections, and may loan their own resources, proprietary materials are always excluded from interlibrary loan.

The Frugal Librarian recommends that common forms of information collected by the business library should organized as simply as possible. For example, the catalogs of competitors can be shelved in alphabetical order by the name of the firm.

Books

Directory of Special Libraries and Information Centers. 23rd ed. Detroit: Gale Research, 1998, 2 vols. This multi-volume directory is of considerable value in identifying other special libraries, and a good resource for comparison and interlibrary loan.

Euromonitor Staff. *European Directory of Business Information Libraries.* Detroit: Gale Research, 1990.

Managing Small Special Libraries. Washington, DC: Special Libraries Association, 1992. 106p.

Matarazzo, James. *Knowledge & Special Libraries.* Woburn, MA: Butterworth-Heinemann, 1998. 265p.

Mount, Ellis. *Special Libraries & Information Centers,* 3rd ed. Washington, DC: SLA, 1995.

White, Herbert. *Managing the Special Library: Strategies for Success Within the Larger Organization.* New York, Macmillan, 1984. 152 p.

Medical, Health Sciences, and Institutional Libraries

Medical and health sciences libraries may be found in hospitals, clinics, health centers, medical research laboratories, universities, and wherever there is a need for literature and information associated with the biomedical and health sciences. Because medical libraries can include resources on dentistry, pharmacology, nursing and public health in addition to the medical sciences, they can be expected to be highly specialized, and a knowledge of the literature and background in the health sciences would be of critical importance to the medical library manager serving the professional and research staff.

The Medical Library Association in the U.S. offers a certification program for librarians working in medical institutions, and sponsors continuing education courses to keep members current on trends and management of the collection. Special training has also been developed for medical library technical assistants. The National Library of Medicine is a key resource to all medical libraries in terms of its role as the center for a nationwide computerized network of resources, strengthened by the participation of major medical research libraries located throughout the nation. Research sharing is a key element in medical library service today. Many medical libraries are also active participants in regional and local multitype library systems, lending valuable backup in their special area of emphasis.

Many hospitals, clinics and public health centers maintain libraries designed for patient use. In the past these may have had a recreational character, but with the shorter duration of the average patient stay, today these resources are more likely to be a of therapeutic nature, used by therapists or other staff to aid the patient in recovery and adjustment. An increasing number of corporations are also establishing general health care collections for their employees, because of the value of this information in preserving good health. Recreational collections are more likely to be found in extended care facilities, and it is here where the library manager may not require special training in the health sciences, although an understanding of the mission of the institution and the needs of the residents or users will be important. Institutions devoted to resident or out-patient care are also likely to have professional or technical collections, and if this is the case, the library manager

Associations for Business Libraries

A primary resource in the U.S. is the:

Special Libraries Association
1700 18th St.
Washington, DC 20009-2514
Tel. 202/234-4700
Fax 202/265 9317
E-mail sla@sla.org
Web: www.sla.org

Special Libraries is the SLA's journal, and the organization also issues publications, schedules an annual conference and offers special training for its members, especially for those in areas such as the physical, biological, technical and social sciences, the humanities and business. Membership in the SLA is an excellent way to build a network of contacts to assist in research, as well as a means to keep current with new products, services and trends. SLA has chapters in many states and metropolitan areas that offer programs and sponsor resource sharing activities.

Business library managers in other nations can gain assistance from the

International Federation for Information and Documentation (FID)
Box 90402
2509 LK
The Hague, Netherlands
314-0671
Fax 314-0667
e mail fid-geo2.geomail.org

Many nations also have special library associations. For example, in the United Kingdom, the key organization is the

Association for Information Management (ASLIB)
Information House
20-24 Old Street
London EC1V 9AP
Fax 71-430-0514

The International Literary Market Place (Bowker, annual) lists many of these organizations.

should rely on an advisory committee for the selection and maintenance of this portion of the library.

Volunteers are often used to good advantage in many institutional libraries. Resident care may require the book trucking of small collections into wards and rooms, and maintaining deposit collections.

Institutional Libraries

The collections of institutional libraries will depend on the mission of the institution and its users, but they are customarily more specialized. For example, a collection for a nursing home or hospice would most certainly contain large print materials, audio books, and would likely have many resources that would be inspirational in content. Many of these institutions are affiliated with religious denominations, and their collections are likely to reflect their values and philosophies.

Veterans' hospitals, rehabilitation facilities, and correctional institutions each have unique functions, and if the library manager is not familiar with them, the best recourse is to assemble an advisory committee to develop guidelines for the collection and services.

Books

Dale, Peter. *Guide to Libraries & Information Sources in Medicine & Health Care,* 2nd ed. Mahwah, NJ: Erlbaum, Lawrence Associates, 1997. 192p.

Johnson, Mary, and Medical Library Association Staff. *Library Services in Mental Health Settings.* Lanham, MD: Scarecrow Press, 1997. 200p.

Kellerman, Frank P. *Introduction to Health Sciences Librarianship: A Management Handbook.* Westport, CT: Greenwood, 1997. 240p.

Lipscomb, Caroline E., ed. *Information Access and Delivery in Health Sciences Libraries.* Lanham, MD: Scarecrow Press, 1996. 280p.

Richards, Daniel, and Dottie Eakin. *Collection Development and Assessment in Health Sciences Libraries.* Lanham, MD: Scarecrow Press, 1997. 360p.

Wood, M. Sandra. *Reference & Information Services in Health Sciences Librarianship.* Metuchen, NJ: Scarecrow Press, 1994. 394p.

Museum and Historical Society Libraries

Because museums are educational institutions, libraries are essential to the mission of this type of institution. In addition, the museum library can greatly assist the research conducted by the museum's professional curatorial staff. There are a rich variety of museums, including those specializing in art, science, history, natural history, as well as those that specialize in the history of specific professions, institutions, or organizations such as colleges and corporations. The number of museums has greatly increased throughout the world, particularly since the end of World War II. Over 5,000 exist in the United States and Canada, the two nations which appear to have the largest number of such institutions.

Museums perform three major functions: collection, study and communication. The library has a key role in all three functions. Resources are needed to aid curators in the identification of materials the museum collects and in their preservation. The study of these artifacts also depends on a strong and specialized research collection. Finally, the library must be used

Associations for Medical & Institutional Libraries

The Medical Library Association
6 N. Michigan Avenue, Suite 300
Chicago, IL 60602
Tel. 312-419-9094
Fax: 312-419-8950
E-mail: info@malhq.org
Web: www.mlanet.org

The Association is the primary resource for medical and institutional library managers in the U.S. The main purposes of the MLA are to foster medical and allied scientific libraries, promote continuing education and professional growth of health science librarians, and exchange medical literature. The MLA has an active publications program, and they also offer certification and training programs in addition to the sponsorship of regular conferences. They publish the *Bulletin of the Medical Library Association,* a quarterly journal.

The Association of Specialized and Cooperative Library Agencies, which is a division of the ALA (50 E. Huron St., Chicago, IL 60611, Tel. 312/280-4395, Fax: 312/944-8085, E-mail ASCLA@ala.org) is another association which has a particular interest in service to the disabled and to institutions.

Medical library managers in other nations should contact the major medical library in their country for information regarding the address and telephone numbers of relevant library associations.

by the museum's curatorial staff in its educational programs. Exhibits, tours and classes require books, films and assorted other materials to reach different audiences and illuminate the collections. Some museums have strong outreach programs with the schools, and library materials may be essential to aid teachers or external lecturers in interpreting the collections.

Historical societies play an important role through their efforts to preserve books, pamphlets, manuscripts and archives, as well as through their publications programs. Libraries have traditionally been associated with historical societies, and are essential to their research, preservation and educational functions. The United States is considered to have more historical societies than any other nation, and there are estimated to be over 2,400 active societies. State historical societies are among the largest, but there are also numerous local and private historical societies and libraries.

Both museums and historical societies collect artifacts as well as books and other documents, and a number of special classification and cataloging systems have been devised to ensure control and ease of access. Great care is exercised in the acquisition of these materials, verifying their authenticity, and in their preservation. Often, these materials are one-of-a-kind, and it would be impossible to replace them. Museum and historical society libraries could use or adapt one of the special classification and cataloging systems for their collection, but it is recommended that a standard system such as DDC or LC be used, to be consistent with other research libraries.

Since preservation is a critical concern in these libraries, care should be taken to use standard archival practices. This includes the use of acid free files and storage boxes, and marking which does not damage the rare documents and other materials likely to be housed in the library. Rare and important books and manuscripts might be preserved through a laboratory process known as deacidification or by microfilming. Preservation is both an art and a science, and the library manager responsible for the museum or historical society will need training or experience in these procedures, besides familiarity, experience or training in history or in the institution's speciality.

Because the collection is likely to be scholarly or highly specialized, the library manager would be well advised to create a committee composed of representatives from the professional curatorial staff to advise on the development of the collection and its preservation.

Books

Ambrose, Tim, and Crispin Paine. ***Museum Basics.*** New York: Routledge, 1992. 196p.

Banks, Paul, and Roberta Pilette, eds. ***Preservation: Policy and Practice.*** Chicago: ALA, 2000. 376p.

Burcaw, G. Ellis. ***Introduction to Museum Work,*** 3rd ed. Walnut Creek, CA: AltaMira Press, 1997. 240p.

Creigh, Dorothy W. ***A Primer for Local Historical Societies,*** 2nd expanded rev. ed. Walnut Creek, CA: AltaMira Press, 1991. 132p.

Fox, Lisa. ***Preservation Microfilming: A Guide for Librarian and Archivists,*** 2nd ed. Chicago: ALA, 1995. 480p.

Hamilton, Marsha. ***Guide to Preservation in Acquisition Processing.*** Chicago: ALA, 1993. 20p.

Tedeschi, Anne C. ***Book Displays: A Library Handbook.*** Ft. Atkinson, WI: Highsmith Press, 1996. 120p.

Associations for Museum & Historical Society Libraries

The American Association of Museums
1225 Eye St., NW, Ste. 200
Washington, DC 20005
Tel. 202/289-1818
Fax: 202/289-6578
Web: www.aam-us.org
is the primary association devoted to the improvement of museums in the United States. The AAM sponsors publications, continuing education and other activities designed to advance museums. Extremely valuable for locating the special collections in museum libraries is the *Official Museum Directory* (Bowker), compiled under the auspices of the AAM.

The Special Libraries Association (p. 85) also has sections and activities which are appropriate for museum and historical society library staff.

Another organization that is pertinent is the
Society of American Archivists
527 S. Wells St., 5th Fl.
Chicago, IL 60607
Tel. 312/922-0140
Fax: 312/347-1452
E-mail: info@archivists.org
Web: www.archivists.org
The purpose of the SAA is to promote sound principles of archival economy and facilitate cooperation among archivists and archival agencies. They publish *The American Archivist,* a biennial journal.

The American Association for State and Local History
530 Church Street, Ste. 600
Nashville, TN 37219-2325
Tel. 615/255-2971
Fax: 615/255 2979
E-mail: history@aaslh.org
Web: www.aaslh.org
is the key organization devoted to the development of historical societies in the U.S. and Canada. The AASLH offers publications, training and conference programs.

Similar associations exist for library managers in museums and historical societies in other nations. These can be located in the *Encyclopedia of Associations: International Organizations* (Detroit: Gale Research).

Appendix A

UNITED STATES

Alabama Public Library Service
6030 Monticello Dr.
Montgomery, AL 36130 2001
(334) 213-3900

Alaska State Library Archives & Museums
Alaska Department of Education
Division of Library Archives & Museums
State Office Bldg.
P.O. Box 11057
Juneau, AK 99811-0571
(907) 465-2910
Fax (907) 465-2665
E-mail: asl@muskax

Arizona State Library
Department of Library, Archives & Public Records
State Capitol
1700 W Washington, Room 200
Phoenix, AZ 85007-2896
(602) 542-4035
Fax (602) 542-4972

Arkansas State Library
One Capitol Mall
Little Rock, AR 72201-1081
(501) 682-1527
Fax (501) 682-1529

California State Library
914 Capitol Mall
Library & Courts Bldg.
P.O. Box 942837
Sacramento, CA 94237 0001
(916) 654-0183
Fax (916) 654-0064
E-mail: csl-ill@library.ca.gov

Colorado State Library
Colorado Department of Education
201 E Colfax
Denver, CO 80203-1704
(303) 866-6900
Fax (303) 866-6940

Connecticut State Library
231 Capitol Ave.
Hartford, CT 06106
(203) 566-4777
Fax (203) 566-8940

Delaware Dep. of State, Division of Libraries
43 S. DuPont Hwy.
Dover, DE 19901
(302) 739-4748
Fax (302) 739-6787
E-mail: delstlib@hslc.org

State Library of Florida
Division of Library Services, Dept. of State
R A Gray Bldg.
Tallahassee, FL 32399 0250
(904) 487-2651
Fax (904) 922-3678

Georgia Department of Education
Division of Public Library Services
156 Trinity Ave. SW
Atlanta, GA 30303-3692
(404) 657-6220
Fax (404) 651-9447

Hawaii State Public Library System
Office of the State Librarian
465 S King St., Rm. B-1
Honolulu, HI 96813
(808) 586-3704
Fax (808) 586-3715

Idaho State Library
325 W. State St.
Boise, ID 83702-6072
(208) 334-2150
Fax (208) 334-4016

Illinois State Library
300 S Second St.
Springfield, IL 62701-1976
(217) 785-5600
Fax (217) 785-4326

Indiana State Library
140 N Senate Ave.
Indianapolis, IN 46204-2296
(317) 232-3675
Fax (317) 232-3728

State Library of Iowa
E 12th & Grand
Des Moines, IA 50319
(515) 281-4105
Fax (515) 281-3384

Kansas State Library
State Capitol, 3rd fl.
Topeka, KS 66612-1593
(913) 296-3296
Fax (913) 296-6650

Kentucky Dept. for Libraries and Archives
300 Coffee Tree Rd., Box 537
Frankfort, KY 40602-0537
(502) 875-7000
Fax (502) 564-5773

State Library of Louisiana
760 N. Third St.
Baton Rouge, LA 70821 0131
(504) 342-4913
Fax (504) 342-3547

Maine State Library
LMA Bldg.
State House Sta. 64
Augusta, ME 04333-0064
(207) 287-5600
Fax (207) 287-5615

Maryland State Dept. of Education
Div. of Library Development and Services
200 W. Baltimore St.
Baltimore, MD 21201-2595
(410) 767-0434
Fax (410) 333-2507

Massachusetts Board of Library Commissioners
648 Beacon St.
Boston, MA 02215
(617) 267-9400
Fax (617) 421-9833

Library of Michigan
Box 30007
717 Allegan St.,
Lansing, MI 48909
(517) 373-1580
Fax (517) 373-3381 (out of state),
(800) 292-2431 (in state)

Minnesota State Library Agency
Office of Library Development and Services
440 Capitol Square Bldg.
St. Paul, MN 55101
(612) 296-2821
Fax (612) 296-5418

Mississippi Library Commission
1221 Ellis Ave., Box 10700
Jackson, MS 39289-0700
(601) 359-1036
Fax (601) 354-4181
E-mail: mlcref@Solinet.net

Missouri State Library
P.O. Box 387, 600 W. Main
Jefferson City, MO 65102 0387
(314) 751-3615
Fax (314) 751-3612

Montana State Library
1515 E. 6 Ave.
Helena, MT 59620
(406) 444-3115
Fax (406) 444-5612

Nebraska Library Commission
The Atrium, 1200 N St., Ste. 120
Lincoln, NE 68508-2023
(402) 471-2045
Fax (402) 471-2083

Nevada State Library and Archives
100 Stewart Street
Carson City, NV 89710
(702) 687-8313
Fax (702) 687-8311

New Hampshire State Library
20 Park St.
Concord, NH 03301-6314
(603) 271-2392
Fax (603) 271-2205

New Jersey State Library
Dept. of Education
185 W. State St.
Trenton, NJ 08625-0520
(609) 292-6200
Fax (609) 984-7900

New Mexico State Library
325 Don Gaspar St.
Santa Fe, NM 87501-2777
(505) 827-3800
Fax (505) 827-3888

New York State Library
Rm. 10C34, C.E.C.
Empire State Plaza
Albany, NY 12230
(518) 474-5930
Fax (518) 474-2718

State Library of North Carolina
109 E. Jones St.
Raleigh, NC 27601-2807
(919) 733-2570
Fax (919) 733-8748

North Dakota State Library
Liberty Memorial Bldg.
604 E. Blvd., Capitol Grounds
Bismarck, ND 58505-0800
(701) 328-2490
Fax (701) 328-2040

State Library of Ohio
65 S. Front St., Room 510
Columbus, OH 43215-4163
(614) 644-7061
Fax (614) 466-3584
E-mail: sloadm@slonet.ohio.gov

Oklahoma Dept. of Libraries
200 N.E. 18th St.
Oklahoma City, OK 73105 3298
(405) 521-2502
Fax (405) 525-7804

Oregon State Library
250 Winter St. NE
Salem, OR 97310-0640
(503) 378-4243
Fax (503) 588-7119

State Library of Pennsylvania
Walnut St. & Commonwealth Ave.
Box 1601
Harrisburg, PA 17105
(717) 772-3265
Fax (717) 783-2070

Rhode Island Dept. of State Library Services
300 Richmond St.
Providence, RI 02903-4222
(401) 277-2726
Fax (401) 831-1131

South Carolina State Library
1500 Senate St., Box 11469
Columbia, SC 29211
(803) 734-8666
Fax (803) 734-8676

South Dakota State Library
800 Governors Dr.
Pierre, SD 57501-2294
(605) 773-3131
Fax (605) 773-4950

Tennessee State Library & Archives
403 Seventh Ave., N
Nashville, TN 37243-0312
(615) 741-2451
Fax (615) 741-6471
E-mail: egleaves@tbr.state.tn.us

Texas State Library
1201 Brazos
Box 12927, Capitol Sta.
Austin, TX 78711
(512) 463-5460
Fax (512) 463-5436

Utah State Library
2150 S. 300 W, Suite 16
Salt Lake City, UT 84115
(801) 466-5888
Fax (801) 533-4657

Vermont State Dept. of Libraries
State Office Bldg., Post Office
Montpelier, VT 05609-0601
(802) 828-3265
Fax (802) 828-2199
E-mail: pklinck@dol.state.vt.us

The Library of Virginia
11 St. at Capitol Sq.
Richmond, VA 23219
(804) 786-8929
Fax (804) 786-5855

Washington State Library
PO Box 42460
Olympia, WA 98504-2460
(360) 753-5590
Fax (360) 586-7575

West Virginia Library Commission
Science and Cultural Center
Charleston, WV 25305
(304) 558-2041
Fax (304) 558-2044

Wisconsin Dept. of Public Instr.
Division of Library Services
125 S. Webster St., Box 7841
Madison, WI 53707-7841
(608) 266-2205
Fax (608) 267-1052

Wyoming State Library
2301 Capitol Ave.
Cheyenne, WY 82002-0006
(307) 777-7281
Fax (307) 777-6289

CANADA

Alberta Dept. of Culture & Multiculturalism
Libraries and Community Development Branch
16214-114th Ave.
Edmonton, Alberta T5M 2ZS
(403) 427-2556
Fax (403) 427-0263

British Columbia Ministry of Municipal Affairs
Library Services Branch
800 Johnson Street, 3rd floor
Victoria, BC V8V 1X4
(604) 356-1791
Fax (604) 387-4048

Manitoba Culture, Heritage & Citizenship
Public Library Services Branch
1525 First Street, Unit 200
Brandon, Manitoba R7A 7A1
(204) 726-6590
Fax (204) 726-6868

New Brunswick Library Service
Maryville Pl., 2nd floor, Room 210
PO Box 6000
Fredericton, NB E3B 5H1
(506) 453-2354
Fax (506) 453-2416
E-mail: NBLS@UNB.CA

Newfoundland Provincial Public Library Services
Arts and Culture Center
Allandale Road
St. John's, Newfoundland A1B 3A3
(709) 737-3964
Fax (709) 737-3009

Northwest Territories Public Library Services
PO Box 1100
Hay River, Northwest Territories X0E 0R0
(403) 874-6531
Fax (403) 874-3321

Nova Scotia Provincial Library
3770 Kempt Rd.
Halifax, NS B3K 4X8
(902) 424-2400
Fax (902) 424-0633
E-mail: inshpl@nshpl.library.ns.ca

Archives of Ontario Library
77 Grenville St., Unit 300
Queen's Park
Toronto, Ontario M7A 2R9
(416) 327-1553
Fax (416) 327-1999

Prince Edward Island Provincial Library Service
PO Box 7500
Morell, Prince Edward Island C0A 1S0
(902) 961-3200
Fax (902) 961-3203
E-mail: pghholma@upei.ca

Saskatchewan Provincial Library
1352 Winnepeg Street
Regina, Saskatchewan S4P 3V7
(306) 787-2972
Fax (306) 787-8866

Government of Yukon, Libraries & Archives Div.
Yukon Place, 80 Range Road
PO Box 2703
Whitehorse, Yukon Y1A 2C6
(403) 667-5309
Fax (403) 667-4253

Dewey Decimal Classification

Appendix B

000	**Generalities**	500	**Natural sciences & mathematics**
010	Bibliography	510	Mathematics
020	Library & information science	520	Astronomy & allied sciences
030	General encyclopedic works	530	Physics
040		540	Chemistry & allied sciences
050	General serials & their indexes	550	Earth sciences
060	General organizations & museology	560	Paleontology; Paleozoology
070	News media, journalism, publishing	570	Life sciences
080	General collections	580	Botanical sciences
090	Manuscripts & rare books	590	Zoological sciences
100	**Philosophy & psychology**	**600**	**Technology (Applied sciences)**
110	Metaphysics	610	Medical science; Medicine
120	Epistemology, causation, humankind	620	Engineering & allied operations
130	Paranormal phenomena	630	Agriculture
140	Specific philosophical schools	640	Home economics & family living
150	Psychology	650	Management & auxiliary services
160	Logic	660	Chemical engineering
170	Ethics (Moral philosophy)	670	Manufacturing
180	Ancient, medieval, Oriental philosophy	680	Manufacture for specific uses
190	Modern Western philosophy	690	Buildings
200	**Religion**	**700**	**The Arts**
210	Natural theology	710	Civic & landscape art
220	Bible	720	Architecture
230	Christian theology	730	Plastic arts; Sculpture
240	Christian moral & devotional theology	740	Drawing & decorative arts
250	Christian orders & local church	750	Painting & paintings
260	Christian social theology	760	Graphic arts; Printmaking and prints
270	Christian church history	770	Photography and photographs
280	Christian denominations & sects	780	Music
290	Other & comparative religions	790	Recreational & performing arts
300	**Social sciences**	**800**	**Literature and rhetoric**
310	General statistics	810	American literature in English
320	Political science	820	English & Old English literatures
330	Economics	830	Literatures of Germanic languages
340	Law	840	Literatures of Romance languages
350	Public administration	850	Italian, Romanian, Rhaeto-Romanic
360	Social services; association	860	Spanish & Portuguese literatures
370	Education	870	Italic literatures; Latin
380	Commerce, communications, transport	880	Hellenic literatures; Classical Greek
390	Customs, etiquette, folklore	890	Literatures of other languages
400	**Language**	**900**	**Geography & history**
410	Linguistics	910	Geography & travel
420	English & Old English	920	Bibliography, genealogy, insignia
430	Germanic languages; German	930	History of ancient world
440	Romance languages; French	940	General history of Europe
450	Italian, Romanian, Rhaeto-Romanic	950	General history of Asia; Far East
460	Spanish & Portuguese languages	960	General history of Africa
470	Italic languages; Latin	970	General history of North America
480	Hellenic languages; Classical Greek	980	General history of South America
490	Other languages	990	General history of other areas

Appendix C

A	General Works
B–BJ	Philosophy. Psychology
BL–BX	Religion
BL, BM,	Religion: Religions, Hinduism,
BP, BQ	Judaism, Islam, Buddhism
BX	Religion: Christian Denominations
C	Auxiliary Sciences of History
D	History: General and Old World (Eastern Hemisphere)
E–F	History: America (Western Hemisphere)
G	Geography. Maps. Anthropology. Recreation
H–HJ	Social Sciences: Economics
HM–HX	Social Sciences: Sociology
J	Political Science
K	Law (General)
KD	Law of the United Kingdom and Ireland
KDZ, KG–KH	Law of the Americas, Latin America and the West Indies
KE	Law of Canada
KF	Law of the United States
KK–KKC	Law of Germany
L	Education
M	Music
N	Fine Arts
P–PA	General Philology and Linguistics Classical Languages and Literatures
PA Supplement	Byzantine and Modern Greek Literature
PB–PH	Modern European Languages
PG	Russian Literature
PJ–PM	Languages and Literatures of Asia, Africa, Oceania. American Indian Languages. Artificial Languages.
P–PM Supp.	Index to Languages and Dialects
PN, PR, PS, PZ	General Literature. English and American Literature. Fiction in English. Juvenile belles lettres.
PQ, Part 1	French Literature
PQ, Part 2	Italian, Spanish, and Portuguese Literatures
PT, Part 1	German Literature
PT, Part 2	Dutch and Scandinavian Literatures
P–PZ	Language and Literature Tables
Q	Science
R	Medicine
S	Agriculture
T	Technology
U	Military Science
V	Naval Science
Z	Bibliography. Library Science

Interlibrary Loan Form

Appendix D

Request no.:   Date: Need before: Notes:

Call No.

Patron Information:

Book author; OR. Serial title, volume, issue, date, pages; OR, Audiovisual title:

Book title, edition, imprint, series; OR, Article author, title: ☐ This edition only

Verified in: AND/OR, Cited in:

ISBN, ISSN, LCCN, or other bibliographic number:

Request complies with   Authorization_____

( ) 108(g) (2) Guidelines (CCG)
( ) other provisions of copyright law (CCL)   Telephone: _____

TYPE OF REQUEST:
( ) LOAN; WILL PAY FEE _____
( ) PHOTOCOPY; MAX. COST $ _____
( )

LENDING LIBRARY REPORT: Date _____
Date shipped_____ Shipped via_____
Insured for $_____ Charges $ _____
DUE_____ ( ) Return insured
Packing requirements _____
REQUIREMENTS: ( ) Library use only
( ) Copying not permitted ( ) No renewals
( ) _____

NOT SENT BECAUSE: ( ) In use ( ) Lacking
( ) Not owned ( ) At bindery ( ) Cost exceeds limit
( ) Non Circulating ( ) Not found as cited
( ) Not on shelf ( ) Poor condition ( ) Lost
( ) Lacks copyright compliance ( ) On order
( ) Vol./issue not yet available ( ) On reserve
( ) In process ( ) Rerequest on
( ) Hold placed
( ) Estimated cost of: Loan $ _____
Photocopy $ _____ Microfilm/fiche $ _____
( ) Prepayment required

BORROWING LIBRARY RECORD:
Date received _____ Date returned _____
Returned via_____Insured for $ _____
Payment provided $ _____

RENEWALS:
Date requested _____
New date due _____
Renewal denied _____
ALA INTERLIBRARY LOAN FORM

Library-Related Resources on the Internet

Appendix E

The Internet is a massive network of computers that was initiated by the U.S. federal government and several major academic institutions to ensure high speed digital communication could be preserved in the event of a nuclear disaster. It became a primary method for the participating institutions to share information, and the application quickly spread throughout the world. Because of breakthroughs in computer technology, it is now possible for virtually any library or individual to use the Internet.

The Internet offers many resources of particular value to the small library. Reference resources such as special databases, the text of recent legislation, catalogs of library suppliers and publishers, directories, and the holdings of many major libraries, including the Library of Congress can be found there. You can add your library to the mailing list of a rich variety of information providers, and participate in discussion groups on problems and issues that affect your library. Through electronic mail you can send messages to other libraries throughout the world. Most important of all, virtually all of these resources are free!

Unfortunately, there are several requirements your library will need to use the Internet. First and foremost, you will need a computer and a modem to communicate with the Internet. Second, you need a service provider to connect you to this network, and some computer software to make this process convenient. Last, but not least, you will need some training to permit you to make effective use of the Internet, and to learn what is available on it.

Selecting a Computer for the Internet

Either an Apple Macintosh or an IBM compatible personal computer (PC) equipped with Microsoft Windows 3.1 or Windows 95 and a modem with a transmission speed of at least 9600 baud can be used to access the Internet. However, your ability to rapidly access data on the Internet will be dramatically affected by the power, features, and capacity of the computer you use. If you are a novice in using and selecting computers, there are several resources available to you. First, there are several books listed at the end of this introduction that can provide guidelines. Second, your cooperative library system or state library may be able to offer consultant assistance. You can also attend training programs offered by your local college or your state library association. Some libraries rely on the advice of their computer sales representative. While this is an option, it should be realized that the salesperson may have a bias in favor of a product she or he represents.

Connecting with the Internet

Internet service providers are numerous in most areas in the U.S. The service is provided by major corporations such as America Online, Compuserve, and

AT&T. Many local entrepreneurs also offer access, and your local telephone directory will list them. Some universities and library cooperative networks offer access.

Internet service providers offer a variety of service options and payment plans, and you will need to ask for quotes and compare the prices. Your selection will depend on the volume of usage you anticipate, and the features you want. This will be difficult to determine without experience on the Internet, and insight into the services that are available. Your best recourse is to seek the advice of other library managers who are using the Internet, consultant advice from your library system or state library, or to defer selection until you have obtained some training.

You will also need to select software for accessing the Internet, and there are many choices, depending on the hardware you have selected, and the size of your budget. Many Internet service providers will offer software packages they recommend for individuals and organizations that subscribe to their service. Some software can also be "downloaded" or transferred from the Internet into your computer at no cost. These may be satisfactory, but until you have gained training or gained the advice of your colleagues or consultants, you may wish to defer selection.

Training for the Internet

There are a multitude of sources for Internet training. Most cooperative library systems and state library agencies maintain calendars listing training opportunities. State and provincial library associations, as well as the national associations, offer seminars, conference programs, and publications. Local community colleges and universities also offer training, although their courses are unlikely to be library-specific. Nonetheless, the basic courses of the general features of the Internet may be very useful. Some large computer store chains and service providers offer training, but care should be taken to ensure the training is not offered primarily to promote a specific product or service.

Selected Library-Related Resources

Compiled by Lisa Guedea

NOTE: Subscription instructions vary depending on the system used to administer the list (listserv, listproc, majordomo, etc.). For more information on a specific discussion group, including how to subscribe and who may subscribe, search for it by name on the Web sites referenced below.

Web Resources for Finding Electronic Discussion Groups by Subject and/or Keyword:

Kabacoff, Rob. Search for Interest Groups." Inter-Links Internet Access."
http://alabanza.com/kabacoff/Inter-Links/ (15 March 2000).

Kovacs, Diane K. "Directory of Scholarly and Professional E-Conferences."
http://n2h2.com/KOVACS/ (15 March 2000).

Southwick, Scott. "LISZT, the mailing list directory."
http://www.liszt.com/ (15 March 2000).

Walter Shelby Group. "TILE.NET/LISTS, The Reference to Internet Discussion & Information Lists."
http://www.tile.net/lists/ (15 March 2000).

Books

Hollands, William D. *Teaching the Internet to Library Staff and Users: 10 Ready-To-Go Workshops That Work.* New York: Neal-Schuman, 1999. 208p.

Janes, Joseph, et al. *The Internet Public Library Handbook.* New York: Neal-Schuman, 1998. 300p.

Semenza, Jenny Lynne. *The Librarian's Quick Guide to Internet Resources.* Ft. Atkinson, WI: Highsmith Press, 1999. 88p. A clearly written introduction to the basic tools and procedures, together with 500+ websites organized into 76 subject categories.

Imhoff, Kathleen. *Making the Most of New Technology.* New York: Neal Schuman, 1995. 150p.

Saffady, William. *Introduction to Automation for Librarians,* 4th ed. Chicago: ALA, 1999. 416p.

Swan, James. *Automating the Small Library.* Ft. Atkinson, WI: Highsmith Press, 1996. 120p.

Library-Related Electronic Discussion Groups

AALISA-L	African-American Library and Information Sciences Issues
AALLC	Asian American Law Librarian Caucus
ACRL	Association of College and Research Libraries
ADAPT-L	Library Adaptive Technology
ADLIB-SYS	Library and Administrative Automated Systems
AFAS-L	African American Studies and Librarianship
ALA-WO	ALA Washington Office Update
ALANEWS	ALA News Releases
ALAOIF	ALA Office for Intellectual Freedom
ALASC-L	ALA Student Chapters
ALCTS	Association for Library Collections and Technical Services
ALISJOBS	Library & Information Science Job Postings
ALSC-L	Association for Library Service to Children
ANSS-L	Library Issues among Specialists in Anthropology, Sociology & Related Fields
APALA-L	Asian Pacific American Librarians Association
ARCLIB-L	Architecture School Librarians' Group
ARLIS-L	Arts Libraries Discussion List
ASCLA-L	Association for Specialized and Cooperative Library Agencies
ASSOC-L	Associates: The Electronic Library Support Staff Journal
ATLANTIS	American Theological Library Discussion List
AXSLIB-L	Disability Access to Libraries
BI-L	Bibliographic Instruction Discussion Group
BIBSOFT	Discussion of Software for Citations and Bibliographies
BLACKLIB	Conference of Black Librarians
BUSLIB-L	Business Libraries Discussion List
CALA	Chinese American Librarians Association
CALIBALL	All California Librarians
CALIBK12	California Library Media Teachers
CALIBPUB	California Public Librarians
CARLIS-L	Canadian Art Libraries Society
CATALOGING	Library Cataloging
CDROM-L	Hardware and Software Issues Related to the Design, Production, and Use of CD-ROM
CIRCPLUS	Library Circulation Issues
CJC-LA	CRL's Community and Junior College Libraries Section

COLLDV-L	Library Collection Development List
COMLIB-L	Communications Librarians
CONSALD	Committee on South Asian Libraries and Documentation
CONTENT	Content Analysis
COOPCAT	Library Cooperative Cataloging
DOCDEL-L	Document Delivery
DORAL	Development Officers of Research Academic Libraries
EDLIB-L	Academic Education Librarians
EJBLACK	Electronic Journal for Black Librarianship
ELDNET-L	American Society of Electrical Engineering Libraries Division Network
ENVREFLIB-L	Environmental Reference Librarians
EQUILIBR	Diversity in Libraries
ERL-CDROMS	Library Networked CDROMs
EXLIBRIS	Rare Book and Manuscript Librarianship
FEDREF-L	The Federal Reference Librarians
FEDSIG-L	Federal Electronic Data Special Interest Group
FEM-BIBLIO	Discussion of Books Relating to Women and/or Spirituality
FISC-L	Fee-Based Information Service Centers in Academic Libraries
FORO-L	Transborder Libraries Forum/Foro trinacional de bibliotecas
GAY-LIBN	The Gay/Lesbian/Bisexual Librarians Network
GO4LIB-L	Library Gophers
GOVDOC-L	Government Documents & Depository Library issues
GSAFD	Library Subject Access To Fiction
GSLISTEC	Library & Information Science Technology Issues
H-INFOED	Education for Health Information & Library Work
HLICP	Hospital Library Internet Connection Project
HMATRIX-L	Online Health Resources
IFREEDOM	Intellectual Freedom and Censorship Issues in Canada
ILL-L	Interlibrary Loan
ILL_LIST	Interlibrary Loan
INDEX-L	Indexing
LALA-L	Latin Americanist Librarians Announcements
LAMA	Library Administration and Management Association
LATAM-INFO	Latin American Studies

LAW-LIB	Law Librarians
LAWLIBREF-L	Law Library Reference Queries
LCCN	Library of Congress Cataloging Newsline
LEXPSYS	Library Expert Systems
LEZBRIAN	Lesbian and Bisexual Women Library Workers
LIB-COMP	Patron-Related Library Computing
LIBADMIN	Library Administration and Management
LIBDEV	Academic and Research Library Development
LIBEX-L	Exhibits and Academic Libraries
LIBJOBS	Library and Information Science jobs
LIBPER-L	Library Personnel Issues
LIBPWR	National Library Power Program
LIBRARY	General News and Information of Interest to Libraries & Librarians
LIBREF-L	Library Reference Issues
LIBSUP-L	Library Support Staff
LIBTECH	Library Technical Support
LIS-L	Library and Information Science Students
LISA-L	Library Student Assistants in Academic or Public Libraries
LITA-L	Library and Information Technology Association
LITANEWS	Library & Information Technology Assn Newsletter
LM_NET	School Library Media & Network Communications
MCJRNL	Journal of Academic Media Librarianship
MEDIALIB	Media Services in Libraries
MEDLIB-L	Medical and Health Sciences Libraries
MELANET-L	Middle East Librarians Association
MLAIBMLA	International Bibliography in Academic Libraries
NATRESLIB-L	Natural Resources Librarians and Information
NHC-SLA	Special Libraries Association Natural History Caucus
NNEWS	Library and Information Resources on the Internet
NORNFP-L	Library Cooperation
NOVELIST	Librarians' Forum on Literature in English
NRLIB-L	Natural Resources Librarians and Information Specialists
OCCLIB-L	Discussion of issues pertaining to Ontario Community College Libraries
OFFCAMP	Off-Campus Library Services List
OUTLIB-L	Outreach Librarians
POLLIB-L	Polar Libraries/Bibliographic Databases

POPCULIB	Popular Culture Resources in Libraries
PUB-ADV	Citizen Advocacy for Public Libraries
PUBLIB	Public Libraries and the Internet
PUBLIB-NET	Public Libraries
PUBYAC	Children and Young Adult Librarians
RLGAMSC	Research Libraries Group
SCIT-BIB	Studies in Communication and Information Technology Bibliography
SEALIB	Southeast Asian Librarians Forum
SERIALST	Serials in Libraries
SLA-TEL	Special Libraries Association: Telecommications. Division
SLAJOB	Special Libraries Association: Employment Opportunities
SNOWBIRD	Library Leadership Issues Discussion List
SOCSCI-L	Special Libraries Association: Social Science Division
SOLOLIB-L	Solo Librarians
SSLIB-L	Social Science Libraries
STS-L	Science and Technology Librarians
STUMPERS-L	Difficult Reference Questions
TESLA	Technical Standards for Library Automation
VETLIB-L	Veterinary Medicine Library Issues and Information
WHSCL-L	Health Sciences Library Discussion
YALSA-L	Young Adult Library Services Association

Electronic Discussion Groups Focusing on Libraries Outside of North America

AW4LIB-L	Australian Web Librarians
BIBLIO-FR	Library Subjects and Subject Related to the Use of Networked Information and Digital Libraries (Discussion is in French)
EALCWWW	East Asian Libraries Cooperative
ELAG-L	Library Automation in Europe
INETBIB	Internet usage in German or German-speaking libraries
KUTUP-L	Turkish Libraries
LIB-L	German and German-speaking libraries
LIBER-PILOT	European research libraries
LIS-BAILER	Departments of Information and/or Library Studies in the U.K.
LIS-LINK	UK-based general Library and Information Science news and discussion
LIS-LAW	UK-based legal information & law libraries
MEDIBIB-L	Medical and health science librarians in Germany, Austria and Switzerland
UNIVLIBE	University Libraries in Belgium
WAIN	Western Australian Information Network

Appendix F

The following events can be used to further promote the library throughout the year. Two other good resources that list many other library-related events are *Chase's Annual Events* (New York: Contemporary, Annual) and *The Librarian's Engagement Calendar* (Ft. Atkinson, WI: Highsmith Press, Annual).

January	National Hobby Month
February	Black History Month and American History Month
March	Women's History Month
March 1–7	Return the Borrowed Books Week
April	National Library Week is usually celebrated during this month, but the week changes. For example, NLW will fall during April 13–19 in 1997, and April 19–25 in 1998. Call the American Library Association (312-944-6780) to determine specific dates for subsequent years.
	Thank You School Librarian Day is usually observed on Wednesday during NLW.
	International Special Librarian Day is usually observed on Thursday during NLW.
April 2	International Children's Book Day (Birthday of Hans Christian Andersen)
May	Older Americans Month
	Asian Pacific American Heritage Month
June	Gay and Lesbian Book Month
June 1–7	International Volunteers Week
September	Hispanic Heritage Month (September 15-October 15)
	Library Card Sign-up Month
	National Literacy Month
	Banned Books Week. This is usually the last week in September, but it occasionally changes. Call the American Booksellers Association (914-631-7800) to determine specific dates.
October	Computer Learning Month
	National Storytelling Month
	International Book Fair Month
November	American Indian Heritage Month
November 1	National Author's Day
	National Children's Book Week, always the week prior to the week of Thanksgiving.
November 25	Andrew Carnegie's Birthday
December	Universal Human Rights Month

Index

A

AACR2 See Anglo-American Cataloging Rules
abstracts 46
acid free paper 31
acquisitions systems 16
ADA See Americans With Disabilities Act
administration 10
almanacs 45
American Archivist 87
American Association for State & Local History 87
American Association of Law Librarians 6
American Association of Law Libraries 83
American Association of Museums 87
American Association of School Librarians (AASL) 79
American Bar Association 83
American Libraries 6
American Library Association 3, 6
American Library Directory 9, 13
American Library Trustees Association 75
Americans with Disabilities Act (ADA) 39, 55
Anglo-American Cataloging Rules 21
anti-sway bracing 38
architect selection 40
archival practices 87
Association for Information Management 85
Association for Library Service to Children 80
Association of Specialized and Cooperative Library Agencies 86
atlas cases 38
auctions 66
audiocassettes 26
audiovisual equipment 38
audiovisual materials 26
author dinners 66
automated systems 33
AV Market Place 19

B

back-orders 17
backup reference services 47
bake sales 66
bar codes 30
bequests 65
Bernhard, Genore H. 1
bibliographic citations 17
binding 31
BIP See *Books in Print*
Black History Month 70
board of trustees 72
book card systems 32
book deposit stations 74
book numbers 23
book pockets 30
books-by-mail 74
Books In Print 16, 19, 31
bookstores 16
Boolean searching 25
borrowers cards 34
Bowker Annual Library and Book Trade Almanac 19
braille materials 55
branch libraries 56
budgeting 11
building programs 9, 36
bulletin boards 69
Bulletin of the Medical Library Association 6
business libraries 84

C

Canadian Library Association 6
capital budget 73
card catalogs 38
Carnegie, Andrew 4
catalog cards 24
Cataloging in Publication 23
Catholic Library Assoc. 82
Catholic Library World 82
CD-ROMs 47
certified library binderies 31
Chases' Annual Events 70
children's library services 53
Church & Synagogue Libraries 82
Church and Synagogue Library Association 6, 82
church libraries 81
church publishing houses 82
CIP See Cataloging in Publication
circulation procedures 32–34
circulation systems 32–34
collection appraisal 41
collection development policies 8

collection management 10
commissioned salespersons 17
compact disk collections 26
comparative specifications 39
compensation plans 58–59
computerized catalog systems 24
computerized databases 46
computers 17
conflict of interest 74
consultant selection 40
continuous revision 44
conversion processes 33
cooperative library systems 13, 47
Copyright Clearance Center (CCC) 44, 51
copyright restrictions 43
corporate libraries purpose 7
county law libraries 82
county libraries 71
culturally diverse workforce 61
curriculum connections 78
Cutter Table 23

D

date due slips 30
deacidification 31, 87
delivery systems 51
Designing Better Libraries 40
Dewey Decimal Classification System 9, 20, 22, 90
Dewey, Melville 22
dictionaries 45
dictionary stands 38
directories 45
disabilities 54
discrimination in hiring 61
displays in the library 69
distance learning 77
distributors 17
donated materials 25
due process 62

E

earthquake safeguards 38
educational resource centers 76
electronic mail 93
employment applications 61
Encyclopedia of Associations 87
encyclopedias 44
endowments 65

environmental concerns 39
equipment selection 39
evaluating effectiveness 12, 56
events, special 69
exhibits in the library 69

F

fair use 44
fees for services 66
financial development 65
Foundation Directory 67
foundations 67
Franklin, Benjamin 3, 76
Friends of Libraries USA 74
fulfillment services 16
functional specifications 39
fund raising 65
furnishings 38

G

gifts 65
government publications 26, 30
Greenaway plans 17
group services 54
Guide to Reference Books 44
Gutenberg, Johann 3
gutter of the book 31

H

hearing impaired persons 55
historical society libraries 86
human resources 10, 58–63
humidity control 39
HVAC systems 39

I

ILL
   codes 50
   responsibilities 50
   See also interlibrary loan
indexes 46
information brokers 48
Information Science Distance Education Consortium 77
information services coordinator 3
institutional libraries 86
instructional media centers 76
insurance coverage 40
intellectual property 4
interlibrary loan (ILL) 49–52
Interlibrary Loan Practices

Manual 50
Internal Revenue Service 66
International Association of
    Law Libraries 83
International Federation of
    Library Associations 6
*International Literary Market
    Place* 19
International Standard Book
    Number (ISBN) 16
International Standard Serial
    Number (ISSN) 16
Internet 12, 93
    computer requirements
        93
    service providers 93
    software requirements 94
    telecommunications
        requirements 93
    training 94
interviews 61
ISBN   See International
    Standard Book Number

J

job descriptions 10, 58
job titles 2
jobbers 15, 17
John Cotton Dana Awards 69

K

keyword searching 25
Kister, Ken 45

L

LA Record 6
large print books 54
law libraries 82
leadership 64
learning resources centers 76
legal counsel 74
lending library materials 29
Lexis 83
libary design 36–41
libary shelving 37
*Librarian's Engagement
    Calendar* 70
libraries
    defined 2
    history 3
    purpose 4, 7
Library Association 6
Library Binding Institute 31
library bindings 31
library districts 71
Library Literature 46
Library of Congress 50
Library of Congress
    Classification System 9,
    20, 22–23
library service, goals of 5
library suppliers 35
lighting 39
line-item budgeting 11
listservs 12
Literacy Volunteers of
    America 54
Literary Market Place 15, 19
local property taxes 73, 79

Lutheran Church Library
    Association 82

M

Machine Readable
    Cataloging (MARC) 24
magazines 25
maintenance 40
manual circulation systems
    32–33
MARC   See Machine
    Readable Cataloging
marks of ownership 30
marketing 65–67
master cards 22
measurement of library
    service 56
media centers 76
medical libraries 85
Medical Library Association
    6, 85–86
microcomputer
    applications 60
microforms 26
mission statements 8
*Monthly Catalog of U.S.
    Governmnt Publications* 26
multitype cooperative library
    systems 9
municipal libraries 71
museum libraries 86

N

National Children's Book
    Week 70
National Interlibrary Loan
    Code 50
National Library Service 55
National Library Week 70
newsgroups 12
newsletters 68
newspapers 26
noise control 39
nonprint materials 25

O

OCLC See Online Computer
    Library Center
office landscaping 39
Official Museum Directory 87
on approval plans 18
online computer
    databases 46
Online Computer Library
    Center (OCLC) 24, 50
on-order files 16
operating budget 73
order procedures 16
ordering library materials
    14–19
organization charts 10, 58
organizing the collection 9,
    20–28
orientations 54, 69
original cataloging 21
out-of-print materials 15
*Output Measures for Public
    Libraries* 13, 56

outreach 55
overdue fines 34

P

PAC   See Public Access
    Catalog
pamphlets 25
partnerships 51
performance evaluations 62
perimeter shelving 38
periodicals 6
permanent paper 31
personnel problems 62
Philadelphia Library
    Company 3
phonodisks 26
photocharge systems 33
photocopiers 39
photocopying 43
physically challenged patrons
    55
*Planning and Role Setting for
    Public Libraries* 13
plastic covers 30
"post-it" bulletin board 56
preprocessed materials 23
prepublication plans 17
preservation 31, 87
probation periods 61
processing kits 24
processing library materials
    29–35
professional licenses 3
programming for youth 53
promotion of library usage
    65–67
proprietary materials 51, 84
Public Access Catalogs 24
public libaries 71–75
Public Libraries 75
Public Library Association
    (PLA) 75
Public Library Catalog, The 15
public library finances 73
public library policies 72
publisher's catalogs 15
publishers 16

R

radio reading services 55
raffles 66
*Readers Guide to Periodical
    Literature* 46
readers' advisory 54
recognition programs 63
recommended lists 15
recorded books 55
recruiting 60
reference and information
    services 42–48
reference interviews 42
reference networks 47
remainder houses 18
repair, book 31
replacing staff 60
retrospective conversion 34,
    52

S

sale of
    resources 66
    services 66
    surplus equipment 66
sales representatives 17
schedule of hours 10
school boards 77
school libraries 76
school library budgeting 78
school library policies 79
school media centers
    purpose 7
school superintendents 77
Sears List of Subject Headings 21
selection journals 15
selection policies 14
selection resources 15
sign language 55
signage 68
simplified catalogong 21
slipcases 31
small libraries
    roles 4
Society of American
    Archivists 87
space needs 9
special classification
    systems 9
special events 66
special libraries 81–88
Special Libraries 85
Special Libraries Association
    6, 85
Special Libraries 6
spine labels 30
staff attitude 55
staff policy handbooks 58
standard ILL forms 51
standards 78
starter collections 15
state library laws 74
statistics 56
story hours 53
study carrels 38
Subject Headings 21
substandard performance 62
suggestion boxes 56
Superintendent of
    Documents numbers 26
supplies 35
synagogue libraries 81

T

talking books 54
tax support 4
technical equipment 38
telefacsimile for ILL 51
telephone directories 45
termination of staff 62
tours 69
transaction circulation
    systems 32
trustees 72

U

Uniform Resource Location
    (URL) 23

union catalogs 50
union lists of serial
    publications 50
unit card 22
Universal Decimal
    Classification System 20,
    22–23
URL   See Uniform
            Resource Location

usage statistics 8
used book sales 66
user fees 66
user services 10
user surveys 8
user's guides 68

V

vertical files 39
videotape 26
volunteers 61–62

W

*Walford Guide to Reference
    Material* 44

weeding 27
wholesale book suppliers 15
World Guide to Libraries 9, 13

Y

young adult collections 53
Young Adult Library Services
    Association 80